18 MILES FROM EARTH

STORIES FROM
BARBER SHOPS, FRONT PORCHES
AND SUPPER TABLES

WAYNE BRISTOW

ISBN Number 1-57087-544-8

Library of Congress Catalog Card Number 00-133943

Professional Press
Chapel Hill, NC 27515-4371

Manufactured in the United States of America
00 01 02 03 04   10 9 8 7 6 5 4 3 2 1

To Rob

For Whom I Wish Good Memories

Foreword

I FIRST KNEW WAYNE BRISTOW THROUGH HIS father's barber shop on Main Street in Muleshoe, Texas. That's where my granddad got his weekly shave ("shave and a haircut, six-bits!").

And, truth be known, Wayne's father, Clinton Bristow, probably gave me my first store-bought haircut. The elder Bristow came to Muleshoe in 1937 to serve the farmers and ranchers of the Texas High Plains, which was the developing area in the state at that time.

I know for a fact that Wayne got his "gift of gab" from his daddy. As a youngster waiting my turn in Mr. Bristow's shop, I recall listening to him spin one tale after another. Sometimes they were about some old cowboy's latest antics, some dealt with the latest escapades of the town drunk, or the town's "ladies' man." I never knew if the stories were fact or fiction, and it didn't matter.

At that time, the barber shops in small towns like Muleshoe took the place of the six o'clock news, which hadn't been invented yet. I wouldn't be surprised if one segment of barber college at that time gave the future haircutters a lesson in storytelling.

My grandpa, Willie Ellis, who raised me, was a farmer. We started out south of Muleshoe during the Dust Bowl days. He soon saw the light and traded for land north of town, which really blossomed when irrigation wells provided needed water for the crops. When we moved into the Muleshoe ISD, I discovered that Wayne was in my class. By the time we entered high school, we had become good friends.

Wayne had a creative mind even at that time, coming up with a scheme that we could take to the high school principal so we could run an errand downtown, which might develop into a chance to visit the malt shop—either Damron Drug or Western Drug.

Once we decided to join the fad and had our hair bleached at Haywood's Beauty Shop during the noon hour, and arrived back to our fourth-period English class considerably late, and causing a ruckus upon our entry. When the teacher privately told us, "I didn't expect this of you two," Wayne had a great explanation that we were trying out for a part in the senior play which required the fellow to have red hair.

Also by our high school days, some of the older guys who ventured out a bit farther than others, had traveled over to the town of Earth, Texas, to scope out the girls. Later you'd hear one say, "Have you ever been out with one of those Earth women?" Hence the title of this book. I am happy to have collaborated again with my friend, Wayne Bristow. I think our last joint effort was on the 1955 edition of "The Mule Train," our high school yearbook, which was a sellout.

Bill Ellis
Friona, Texas

(Bill Ellis is an award-winning weekly newspaper publisher in the Texas Panhandle, and was the youngest member ever to be elected president of the Panhandle Press Association in 1968.)

Contents

Introduction

MY MATERNAL GRANDFATHER WAS A cowboy-turned-preacher. At a very formative time in my life, we had a housekeeper who was a great storyteller. I grew up in my father's barber shop and became a preacher. For more than 40 years, I've traveled on five continents and many islands. That adds up to a lot of good stories, and even more bad ones. These yarns have covered every imaginable topic: dogs, cats, food, dumb stunts, cowboys and baseball players—you name it. Only now am I becoming properly grateful for all of this. Mine is the heritage of the oral tradition and the extended family.

During the chaos of the '60s, many people in the United States lost this. Today, most of the stand-up comedians who can tell really funny stories without vulgarity are over 70 years old. Television reruns of old situation comedies are surprisingly popular with young people. We instinctively know that laughing and feeling good should go together.

What you are about to read is an unrestrained hodgepodge of reality and embellishment. Your own good judgment will help you decide where one ends and the other starts. Don't be too sure you have it all figured out. When compared to the twists and turns of real life, the exploits of the imagination seem pale. When you're not sure, remember my father's favorite response when I would ask, "Did that really happen?" He would smile and ask, "What do you think?"

Wayne Bristow
June 2000

An Expression of
Appreciation

AS I WROTE THE STORIES THAT MAKE UP *18 Miles From Earth*, I was looking back to a childhood in a small West Texas town that was filled with safety, order, love and laughter. On Memorial Day 2000, on the brink of publishing these stories, I was constrained to pause and remember that many people paid a great price so that a barber's son could experience a childhood such as mine. My parents conceived me in the frightening twilight of a great economic depression and under the shadow of a global conflict. My uncles, Spurgeon King and Bishop Bristow, fought in the South Pacific during World War II. A cousin survived the fighting in North Africa, then was almost cut in two by machine gun fire in Italy. Miraculously, he returned to become the object of our wonder and appreciation. I remember being with my father in a Muleshoe coffee shop and having him point to a man and tell me that he had been held by the Japanese as a prisoner of war. As a little boy, my imagination struggled to comprehend what that meant. Now, I understand that much of the music, many of the movies and most of the stories that I remember so fondly were born out of days of horror, sacrifice and great loss. Somehow, through it all, America laughed and sang. This was the manifestation of the indomitable spirit of our great country. I was privileged to grow up in its heartland. I want to say **"thank you"** to those men and women whose sacrifices allowed me to store up a lot of good memories.

Wayne Bristow
May 2000

The Buttermilk Revival

IN THE WEST TEXAS OF MY CHILDHOOD, IT seemed that it was written in stone: "Every Baptist church shall have a revival meeting during the middle two weeks of August."

Just as surely, it was written, "The women of the church shall attempt to kill the preachers with food, while not being outdone by each other."

No one ever thought about messing with the proven plan for those pre-harvest revivals. Singing and preaching took place every morning and evening. The night gatherings got under way at "dark thirty," in other words, half an hour after sundown. Every farmer and rancher knew that he had been given plenty of time to get all his chores done, and there was no excuse for not having the wife and kids packed onto his pew. The evangelists they came out to hear would have been liked a lot by Abraham Lincoln, who said he wanted to hear a man preach like he was fighting bees.

The ladies of the church fed these preachers real good three times every day, with the last chow down coming just about two hours before preaching time. These arrangements filled visiting evangelists with equal mixtures of delight and fear. More than a few godly men, whose lips had never been wet by hard liquor, ended up digging their own graves with a knife and fork. On their way to glory, they were cheered and helped by the sisters whose names filled the revival meal schedule.

You've got to remember that this was back before everybody and their dog had a telephone. On top of that, houses weren't all that close together. Still, quicker than you can snap your fingers, the next woman on the feeding list knew exactly what her competition had just served up. There was no way that she was about to be bested.

This go-for-broke cooking frenzy guaranteed big tables covered with sugar-cured ham, fried chicken and chicken-fried steak, cracklin' cornbread, yeast rolls made from scratch, fried okra, green onions, sliced home-grown tomatoes, corn on the cob, snapped green beans or black-eyed peas, homemade bread-and-butter pickles, spiced peaches and pickled beets, deviled eggs and stalks of celery spread with pimento cheese (which I've always detested), pan-fried potatoes, cream gravy, collard greens (picked that morning from beside a country road), a rounded bowl of fresh butter (that had been wrapped in cheesecloth and cooled in the cistern), huge goblets of sweet iced tea, side dishes of chow-chow, blackberry or peach cobbler with home-cranked ice cream, freshly iced angel food cake, devil's food cake (guaranteed to put you into chocolate shock) and hot apple pie with cheddar cheese melted on top—all capped off with strong black coffee.

Any preacher who had been around the revival circuit more than once knew the first law of survival: never, never name your favorite food in public. Do this, and the battling cooks would make sure that two weeks later you couldn't look at another serving, let alone eat it.

One summer when I was a kid, a visiting preacher became a legend in our county by forgetting the rule. During the very first service of a protracted meeting, he let it slip that he was really fond of buttermilk. That did it. He was condemned to dealing with that thick, curdled, sour stuff three times every day.

A good revival meeting usually broke loose during its second week, and the preacher was focused on the importance of the second Monday night service in the series when he arrived at a farm home for his supper. "Y'all come on in," beamed the hostess. "I know you like buttermilk. I churned today and I've got scads."

"Oh, boy!" thought the preacher, knowing that he was in serious trouble.

That which he feared came upon him. He had fallen into the hands of the most feared of all preacher feeders. She didn't eat. Instead, she hovered around the table watching for any spare space on anyone's plate. She never asked, and protests were useless. Second helpings were plopped down with machine-like quickness. Once your plate was filled, she made it impossible to make a dent in it. The preacher never had a chance. His glass was endlessly full of buttermilk.

Finally, in utter desperation, he threw up a hand and said, "Ma'am, this is really good buttermilk, but I reckon I've just about had all I can hold."

An hour later, when he stood to preach, he felt even fuller. His heart was pounding, his vision was blurred, his mind was scrambled and just breathing was a chore. Leaning on the pulpit for support, he groaned, "Folks, I'm so full that I can't preach."

A dear sister thought that he meant he was full of the Spirit. She lifted her hands over her head and shouted, "Glory! Hallelujah!"

That busted things loose sure enough. All over the building, folks were shouting and leaping. Before the flustered pastor could restore order, twelve people got saved.

On the way home that night, a smiling deacon turned to his wife and said, "You know, I think what our church probably needs is less preaching and more buttermilk."

Fly Like a Chicken

O F ALL THE THINGS I WANTED TO DO AS A child, I wanted most to fly. Growing up in Muleshoe, it was inevitable. The town is located between Clovis, New Mexico, and Lubbock, Texas. During World War II, there was an Army Air Corps base near both of those cities. This meant that planes were constantly flying over our house. As I watched them, my imagination soared. A steady diet of movies such as *Flying Leathernecks, Thirty Seconds Over Tokyo* and *Flying Tigers* fueled the fantasies.

Saturdays finally pushed me over the edge. During my pre-work years, these were great days. I slept in, leaving the bed only after the Buster Brown® children's radio program was over. As I ate my hot Ralston® and drank my Ovaltine®, the program's jingle played back over and over in my head: "Hi, I'm Buster Brown; I live in a shoe. This is my dog Tige; he lives here, too."

Both the cereal and drink were required brands. I was addicted to the 15-minute radio programs that filled the airwaves on weekday afternoons from the time school was out until supper was ready. They were sponsored mostly by cereal companies. The king was Kelloggs®. A quarter and a boxtop mailed to Battle Creek, Michigan, would get you secret code rings that glowed in the dark, G-Man badges and memberships in the most fantastic clubs imaginable. As appealing as this was, they lost the campaign for my affections to Tom Mix, sponsored by Ralston®, and Captain Midnight, sponsored by Ovaltine®. Once my commitment was made, I was faithful to the core.

After breakfast, it was time for my brother, Dudley, and me to shine our cowboy boots. (We wore shoes only on Sundays.) The shining was required by our mother, who couldn't imagine any proud, decent parent who would allow sons to go downtown on Saturday afternoon without seeing to it that they had polished their boots, had their baths and slicked down their locks with Jeris® Hair Tonic. The polish-and-buff operation took place on the back porch, and was immediately followed by the bath, after which fingernails were inspected.

On very special Saturdays, Mother joined us for the four-block walk to Daddy's barber shop and relieved him of the 90¢ needed for three hamburgers and Cokes® at Collins Café. While shaving a cowboy's neck, Daddy would fume, "Sam Pat and little pistols!

The way y'all spend money, I'm gonna work all day and still won't be able to buy a louse a wrestling jacket."

These protests would always end with his smiling and digging out the coins. As a feigned afterthought, he would hand Dudley and me a shiny half-dollar each, our weekly allowance. Over Mother's objection, I would break my 50¢ piece at the café to get a nickel for the jukebox. "You'll end the day with nothing left for the week."

"No, I won't," I would insist, as my Ink Spots selection competed with the waitress's shouts to the short-order cook.

After the hamburgers were history, Dudley and I would promise to watch the Main Street traffic as we left Mother window shopping at St. Clair's Variety Store to dash over to the Valley Theater.

Saturday always meant a double feature, a "Time Marches On" newsreel, a cartoon and an installment of an adventure serial. We booed if the cartoon wasn't "Tom and Jerry," "Porky Pig" or "Bugs Bunny." My favorite serials were about Captain Midnight, Buck Rogers and The Black Whip (a very interesting woman, even to a small boy). The features followed a strict formula. First there was a detective mystery (*Charlie Chan, The Bowery Boys, Boston Blackie* or *The Thin Man*). Next was the Western, the real reason we were there. My heroes have always been cowboys, and my favorites included Roy Rogers, Gene Autry, Charles Starrett, Jimmy Wakely, Johnny Mack Brown, Bill

Elliott as Red Ryder and Gilbert Roland as the Cisco Kid. He was the only real Cisco Kid as far as I'm concerned.

After the shoot-em-up, I would squint into the bright afternoon sunshine, sneeze and count my money. (Did you ever wonder why coming outside of a dark theater into bright sunshine makes you sneeze?) A nickel blown on the jukebox, 12¢ for the movie ticket and another nickel for popcorn had reduced my funds for the week to 28¢. My next stop was Damron's Drug Store. A cherry Coke® and a choice of two funny books left me only three cents for the next six days, but I had everything I needed to survive.

Since each Saturday had to unfold according to an unwritten but strict schedule, the comic books had to wait until Dudley and I had joined our neighborhood friends in reenacting the matinee action we had just watched. Everybody owned at least two six-shooters with holsters. A lucky few had a Daisy® Red Ryder BB gun. (Yes, our mothers had told all of us, "You'll shoot your eye out.") I wore my guns with the handles pointing forward like Wild Bill Elliott.

Until our mothers called us in at twilight, we rode spirited horses named Trigger, Champion and Tony through canyons and across mountain streams. We were shot and killed and resurrected. The girl next door always insisted that she was The Black Whip. When shooting broke out, she kept saying, "You missed me!"

As I look back on this violence, I don't remember anyone from this group growing up to be a serial killer. Of course, on our Saturday afternoons, the good guys always won.

After a hot bowl of Campbell's® vegetable and beef soup, a grilled cheese sandwich and a glass of milk, I would turn on "Your Hit Parade" and finally settle down with that week's comic books. My tastes ran to super-heroes. My favorites were Batman, Superman and Captain Marvel. Two of these three could fly. By the time I snuggled up in my blanket and quilt, I was ob-sessed with the question, "Is it really possible? Can a man fly without an airplane?"

Finally, one Monday afternoon, two days of this pondering took its toll. I borrowed a clean white dishtowel from Mother's kitchen, spread it on the table and, with an orange crayon, decorated it with a large streak of lightning. As I pinned the cape around my neck and inspected the results in the bathroom mir-ror, I had to admit that, in comparison to Captain Marvel, my muscles left something to be desired; but they had to do.

Now the question was, "If I'm going to fly, where do I take off?"

Convinced that this called for height, I headed for the chicken house. (Even though we lived in town, we had chickens. Today's kids think they come from the freezer in nuggets.) Once I had struggled to the roof of the shed, the dramatic result was assured. The wind always blows in West Texas, so the improvised cape stood out the way any superhero's should.

First, I checked the area. The coast was clear; no one was looking. Then I made the mistake of looking down. It's funny; but it seemed farther down from the top than it had seemed coming up from the bottom. It was too late for thoughts about good judgment. Knowing that my only witnesses were a few puzzled chickens, I took a deep breath, closed my eyes and yelled, "Shazam!"

When I could breathe again, I rolled over on my back, drew my bleeding right knee up under my chin, looked up into the blue sky and thought, "Mother will kill me for tearing my jeans." (That was before you could buy them with the knee already torn.)

I had given it my best shot and had ended up in a cloud of dust. I had screamed like an eagle and flown like a chicken.

Well, Blow Me Down

AROUND MULESHOE IN THE 1940S AND '50S, other than a tornado, our most dreaded natural phenomenon was a sandstorm. Early on a spring or autumn afternoon, a boiling black cloud would rise menacingly on the horizon. At that moment, the wind might be calm and there would be an eerie quietness. A stranger to the area would think that a rainstorm was brewing. Old-timers would just watch the approaching tumult without comment. They knew what was coming, and they were helpless to stop it.

At first, the Chinese elms around the courthouse would just sway gently as the atmosphere took on a surrealistic pinkish-orange color. Even though it was just after lunch, birds would begin flocking in to roost. Goldie, the Palomino stallion in the lot next door to us, would toss his head, paw the ground and roll his eyes. Soft scrapes and thuds could be heard throughout the neighborhood as every woman lowered her windows and closed the doors. Children stopped play and exercised their ingenuity to smuggle dogs into houses.

Usually the bang of an unlatched shed door or the crash of a toppled garbage can announced the full blast of the storm. Trees bent to the breaking point. Tumbleweeds from ranch pastures bounced down Main Street until they collided with approaching pick-ups and cars. Sustained winds of 35 to 45 miles per hour, with gusts up to 50 and 60 mph, rocked parked cars, popped and shredded the flags at the post office, and whistled and moaned around every house in town. Buildings across a street disappeared in a brown fog. Street lamps glowed dimly, and drivers turned on head-lights, groping for lost destinations, now without the help of any discernible landmarks.

The worst imaginable scenario, the one that stuck fear into the heart of every kid, was for one of these black monsters to attack our town during school hours. Our family didn't own a car. It was only three blocks to the elementary school, but that became a mara-thon distance during a sandstorm. Before leaving the schoolhouse, my load was reduced to just the books necessary for that night's homework. I then joined my classmates in tying handkerchiefs over our mouths and noses. As we bolted out of the doors, we must have looked like a horde of small bandits.

No one faced one of these dirt movers. A cross-blast would sting the face with grains that had the driving velocity of tiny darts. An open coat became a billowed sail that could stop the forward progress of a grown man. My stance of choice was to turn my back to the storm and keep it there. Following yard fences, I would back through the swirling dust until I saw the grass of home at my feet. Then it was a short, determined dash to our porch and safety. In spite of my turn-coat tactic, I would arrive with mud in the tears on my cheeks, burning eyes and grit-covered teeth. It was impossible to comb my hair. To attempt to do so dry generated enough static electricity to light the house. To wet it at the bathroom sink created enough mud to clog the drain.

These storms never passed quickly. The wind would continue into the night, causing lights to dim during supper. It was still howling around dark corners as I pulled the bed covers over my head.

Out of this terror was always born the most glorious days I can remember. To wake the morning after a sandstorm was awesome. The air was clean, the sun was brilliant and everyone's mood was buoyant. Even the dirt an inch deep on our inside window sills could not erase the grateful smile from my mother's face. To have been offered a ticket out of town 12 hours earlier would have been irresistible, but now it was too pretty to leave.

One sandstorm could totally change a West Texas landscape. Drifts would cover barbed wire fences and tumbleweeds would pile up, obscuring from view the barn behind them. Rippling mounds of sand added relief to the flat pastures of Bailey County.

On a bright, fresh morning after one of these storms, a cowboy saddled up and rode out to check fences. Two miles from headquarters, he was thrilled to see a beautiful, broad-brimmed hat lying on a freshly formed sand hill. "Finders keepers, losers weepers," he whooped as he dismounted. When he picked up the sombrero, he was stunned to see the hair of a person's head under it. Frantically, he dug away the sand from the imprisoned victim. "Keep digging," the man yelled. "There's a horse under me!"

On the Cutting Edge

ONE OF MY GREATEST REGRETS IS THAT I missed being an adult during an age when a barber shop shave was a daily luxury available to almost every man. At my father's shop, 25¢ would get you a smooth face, the latest news, philosophical interpretation and political commentary. If you were so inclined, you could sleep through the whole thing. The conversation would continue just fine without you, and you would wake up renewed and ready to face any challenge.

Never has so little bought so much. The process was an unhurried exercise of an art. The chair collapsed so that the customer was prone and relaxed, his feet and head resting on leather pads. Stress dissolved as strong hands massaged a menthol cream into the whiskers. While talking, often by this time to a comatose cowboy, Daddy would flip a steaming hot towel from one hand to the other. When he sensed that the wrap would only slightly test a person's tolerance and manhood, he would carefully mold it to the waiting face.

While the heat released vapors from the cream strong enough to open any sinus cavity, a razor would be honed to a hair-splitting edge. This was accomplished in a way that always fascinated me. My father would hold the razor strop, which hung from his chair, in his left hand and with smooth, seemingly casual motions alternate the blade from one side to the other, stroking it against the leather. He would do this without looking, and while engaged intently in a discussion with someone across the room.

When the towel came off, the sleeping customer would stir as the fresh air reacted with the stimulating cream for a bracing rush. The softened beard was almost ready. The lather from the round cake of soap at the bottom of an ageless mug was gently brushed onto the face. Timing was important. The shaving must begin while the whiskers retained the right temperature and moisture.

From this stage on, what happened, and how, made it easy to understand why some barbers had more shave customers than they could handle, and why some got only those poor souls who didn't know any better. The real artist remembered how each client's whiskers grew, their texture and which razor was the right selection for each face. In my book, a close shave with a straight razor in someone else's hand, without a nick, deserves classification as a miracle.

After a careful inch-by-inch examination to be sure no errant facial hair had been missed, Daddy would reach for the tonic guaranteed not only to wake up his subject, but to get his undivided attention. When he slapped on the high-alcohol solution, not-to-be-repeated exclamations often blistered the ceiling plaster. By the time the chair was raised to a sitting position, the customer was alert and talking a blue streak.

Haircuts came and went routinely, but shaves bred legends. My father's first customer every day was Guy Nickels, his one-armed cotton ginner friend. Guy's pickup would be parked in front of the red-and-white barber pole when the doors were unlocked at 7 a.m. He would scan the *Lubbock Avalanche-Journal* while Daddy tied his shoes. During the ensuing discussion of the previous night's baseball games, an agreement would often be struck to go to Clovis, New Mexico, to watch the minor league Pioneers that night. Guy's shave was the official start of the day for both of these good men year after year.

Two shave customers showed up only once each week, but that was enough. They were bachelor brother farmers who greatly resembled bears. Daddy kept a special razor just for them. He would strop this reserved blade on Friday nights. As he anticipated the ordeal ahead, he would announce, "I'm not going to ruin my best razor on their barbed wire."

These unclaimed blessings came to town every Saturday. Their agenda included a shoot-'em-up picture show, a trip to the grocery store and their shaves. The shaves were last because they had to do for church on Sunday morning. After that the men wouldn't go anywhere else where it mattered until the next Saturday.

Daddy was the master, so, of course, he had his occasional apprentice. That's how Roy came to stand behind the shop's third chair. Fresh from a barber college in Lubbock, he had to settle for working on traveling salesmen, troublesome kids that no one wanted and the few locals who never seemed to care for excellence.

Roy had been in town barely a month when he got saved during the summer revival at the Main Street Missionary Baptist Church. The new convert's zeal knew no bounds, and he had a great passion to share the faith. This was his state of mind the afternoon that Odie, our town drunk, wandered into the shop in a haze. "I need a good shave," he muttered.

Pointing down the line, Daddy said, "Roy will take care of you."

Immediately, Roy recognized a sinner in need of help, but he was new at this soul-winning business. As he placed Odie under the hot towel and stropped the razor, he wondered what to say first and when.

Finally, when the lather had been brushed on, he re-membered an arresting question that had been asked by the evangelist who had reached him. Holding the gleaming blade over his prospect's throat, he asked urgently, "Are you ready to die?"

Odie's knee-jerk reaction popped his head up and brought his Adam's apple into brief contact with the razor. After that, no amount of apology or explanation would suffice. However, it was noted that Odie left the shop sober and remained so for several weeks. This was enough to encourage Roy and convince him that often the best roadblock on the broad highway to hell is a good dose of fear.

Chicken Much

FOR A GUY WHO GREW UP AROUND COW-
boys, I sure have spent a lot of time with chickens. One of my earliest memories is the fear of
a big red rooster who had awesome spurs, no sense of
humor and was always between me and the outhouse.

My mother's folks always had three kinds of chickens: laying hens, fryers and that rooster. It was easy
to figure out why the first two were around, but to a
little kid the rooster never made any sense. To this
day, when I hear a cock crow just before dawn, a rush
of nostalgia sweeps over me.

Every spring, the fryers arrived as soft, chirpy baby
chicks. Believe it or not, they came in the mail, ordered from the Sears and Roebuck catalog. The rural
mail carrier would alert my grandfather, and I would
beg to go with him. We were off to the post office, and
an hour later, we were back with big flat boxes full of
air holes and noise.

Just like the okra, corn, tomatoes and black-eyed peas that had recently been planted, I looked on these little feather balls as the start of many a great summer supper. Daily, I watched their progress and guarded them from neighborhood cats. Any chicken lost to a feline marauder meant one less crispy breast to smother in cream gravy.

What these young chickens ate was of great interest to me for two reasons. First, I wanted to see meat on those bones. Secondly, the more they ate, the more new shirts I got.

The feed store on Saturdays was a regular stop for my grandmother and me. What sack she bought was determined by whether or not I liked the design. Once it was empty, she would wash it, cut it according to a pattern purchased at the 5¢ and 10¢ store, and in no time her Singer® sewing machine had added to my wardrobe.

It seemed like eternity, but the day would finally come when the first fryer would meet the fate I had dreamed of for the rooster. This part isn't for the squeamish. My sweet little grandmother wasn't very fast on her feet, but when it was time to catch a chicken, she had an equalizer. No modern kid, munching nuggets at McDonald's, has ever seen what I saw when Mama reached for her long strand of heavy wire with a crook on the business end. Wading into the barnyard crowd, she would quickly make her choice. With a well-aimed swipe and flick of the wrist, the evening's entrée was in her grasp.

Wringing a chicken's neck must be almost a lost art. I'm sure that the SPCA would call for prosecution if anyone should attempt it today. (How *do* they get from the poultry farms to their rendezvous with 33 secret herbs and spices?) When I remember my grandmother's technique, I also remember why she had my undivided attention when I upset her and she said, "I'm going to wring your neck."

While I can't tell you how she did it, I can tell you that she didn't think about it twice. A frantic circle of thrashing wings and the bird had lost all hope. Now he was really in hot water. The two most unpleasant smells in my memory are those of a scalded chicken and singed pinfeathers.

Once these events had taken place, dinner was not far off. Often, this meant that the preacher was coming. Across the southern United States, chicken is still known as "Gospel bird."

One summer, a revival preacher, the local Nazarene pastor and a traveling singer had just polished off one of my grandmother's all-time-best fried chicken dinners. As they relaxed in swings and rocking chairs on the front porch, the old red rooster crowed. Laughing, the evangelist said, "That cock sure sounds proud about something."

"I reckon he oughta be," commented my Uncle Spurgeon. "He's had three sons go into the ministry today."

Knowing how often preachers were served chicken, and guessing that any one of them had about had his fill, a pastor and a mischievous deacon decided to play a joke on an unsuspecting evangelist. When the traveling preacher arrived on Saturday afternoon, he was moved into a spare bedroom at the deacon's farmhouse. "You just got time to wash up. Supper's 'bout ready," he was told.

Fried chicken graced the table at the get-acquainted meal, and the polite guest bragged that it was the best he had ever eaten. To himself, he thought, "Thank goodness, the next meal is breakfast."

To his amazement, breakfast consisted of fried eggs, cat-head biscuits, cream gravy, grits and fried chicken. Like a good boy should, the preacher ate his fill.

After the Sunday morning service, it was back to the deacon's home for lunch. The evangelist couldn't believe it, but there it was—fried chicken. Determined to remain polite and gracious, he commented, "You know, I don't recollect ever having fried chicken for three meals in a row."

"Yeah, I don't understand what's goin' on," declared the grinning deacon. "Those suckers are dyin' faster than we can clean 'em and fry 'em."

After that, people always wondered how a good Southern preacher got to be a strict vegetarian.

Dumb Stunts

MY FATHER DID NOT HAVE A GREAT FOR-
mal education. He made it through the
eighth grade back when depression-era
realities made work on the family farm a necessity. In
spite of this, he was an extremely well-read, intelligent man.

During the pre-TV days of the 1940s, my brother
and I spent hours listening to Daddy read. By the time
I turned 13, we had heard him complete *Ben Hur,
Robinson Crusoe, Black Beauty, The Adventures of Tom
Sawyer, The Adventures of Huckleberry Finn, Lassie
Come-Home,* Will Rogers' autobiography, Zane Grey's
Riders of the Purple Sage, and Will James' *Smoky, The
Cowhorse,* plus stacks of stories from the *Saturday
Evening Post.* He knew world history, really understood
the mechanics of the United States government, and
was a great baseball statistician.

All of this made his stories about childhood exploits even more amazing. Our father was the best, but he never left us any room to believe that he was perfect. In fact, when I really mess up, I still take great comfort in remembering his stories and knowing that smart people can do some pretty dumb things.

His biggest faux pas were the result of an overactive imagination. What he saw, read, heard or thought, cried out to become reality. It just had to be attempted—like the Saturday he managed to buy a Western pulp novel and smuggle it home for reading in the peach orchard. It was about a buffalo hunter who could ride a wild mustang bareback and shoot a rifle with uncanny accuracy, while his steed was running full out.

This started Daddy to thinking. He reasoned that, if the men of the wild west could shoot a rifle from a sprinting mount, surely he could hit a lard bucket on a fence post while firing a shotgun from the back of a plow horse. He remembered finally getting the broad-backed 20-year-old mare up to a lumbering gallop. While his memory was clear about raising the double-barreled shotgun to his right shoulder, he was never able to explain how that old nag covered a hundred yards of country road before he hit the ground at the exact spot where they parted company.

One Saturday morning, he was standing in the back of a wagon, rolling off fence posts for his father to plant in the holes he had spent a week digging.

While the real work was taking place on the ground, Daddy had time to think, a dangerous thing. The day before, he had gone to Anson to watch his younger brother, Bishop, play football. The home team had a cheerleader who turned backward flips while standing flat-footed. He thought that if that guy could do that from the ground, surely he could do it with a four-foot head start from the back of the wagon.

"Great guns, Clinton! Are you all right?" asked his father.

Flat on his back and gasping for breath, Daddy finally managed, "Yes, Dad; I slipped."

It took the full cooperation of an unthinking cousin for him to pull off his number-one dumb stunt. The house and yard were full of kinfolks on a Sunday afternoon. Daddy was standing on the back porch, drinking cool water from the cistern. As he lifted a glass dipper to his lips, he observed his cousin standing in the kitchen. They were separated by a screen door. He thought, "If I hit him in the back of the head with this dipper, that screen would probably keep it from hurting him. The last thing the cousin remembered before kissing the floor was, "Hey, back up to the screen for a minute." For the rest of their lives, they both asked, "Why did I do that?"

Daddy taught me that when smart people do dumb things, they are willing to admit it and can laugh at themselves. Life has taught me that when people who aren't very smart do dumb things, they always have a smart answer that ends up sounding pretty dumb.

This point was proven on a hot summer afternoon in Muleshoe, when one of the town's professional loafers wandered into a blacksmith shop. The sweating smith had just hammered out a red-hot horseshoe. It had barely lost its glow when the ne'er-do-well picked it up. Reacting like he had been hit with an electric cattle prod, he threw the searing metal to the ground.

"That hot?" grunted the blacksmith.

"Nope," said the idler, fighting to regain his poise. "It just don't take me long to look at a horseshoe."

Varmints, Hounds and Hen Houses

A VARMINT IS DEFINED IN A DICTIONARY AS a person or animal regarded as objectionable. As a boy, I had never read that, but I learned early that some varmints have boots and some have paws. Bailey County, Texas, had its share of both.

Only the worst of the two-legged kind would ever call a man's dog a varmint. A rancher or farmer has varmints by the nature of things, but his dog is a matter of choice. Varmints are ranked with demons and horse thieves. Dogs are ranked just below horses and just above wives and children.

Of course, all kinds of varmints and dogs technically qualify for their respective titles. Strictly speaking, skunks, bobcats, badgers and foxes are varmints. In the same way, you'd have to admit that poodles, chihuahuas and schnauzers are dogs. But ask a man in rural West Texas about varmints, and he'll most likely talk about coyotes. Ask him about dogs, and he'll remember some old hound he used to have.

While I know many stories of hounds tangling unwisely with polecats and badgers, I've heard few about their encounters with coyotes. Perhaps this is due to the intelligence of both. This would dictate to each that the other is worth avoiding. In cartoons, coyotes are best known for keeping the price of Acme stock high. In reality, they are known as crafty survivors, capable of living within spitting distance of men, while ignoring roadrunners and thriving on chickens. Good hounds have a propensity for quiet men, pickup trucks and shady porches. Find a West Texas farmer or rancher, and you'll find his dog, whether he's attending a sale, doctoring a sick calf or attending church.

When it comes to hounds, I always think first of Smokey. He belonged to a Baptist deacon who was a cotton farmer. On spring days, that dog could be seen sleeping in the shade of an irrigation pump house, while his master plowed a field. On a cold winter day, he would stretch out beside a table, while the farmhouse kitchen resounded with the click of dominoes. Any day of the week, he would make the trip to Baileyboro General Store facing the wind from the back of a speeding pickup.

Smokey especially liked to attend church. His master's family was faithful at Longview Baptist Church, three miles up the dirt road from their house.

They never missed, nor did Smokey. While the sermon was in progress, he slept on the church's porch. (Now that I think about it, I seldom saw Smokey awake.) On hot summer Sunday mornings, the front door was always open, and the faithful dog could be clearly seen from the pulpit. The pastor would almost get tongue-tied trying to avoid using the word "come." He could just imagine the obedient hound loping down the aisle.

Smokey was no stranger to the dean of varmints. Even the alkali lake west of his master's farm was named Coyote Lake. Nightly, the rural silence was violated by the "yip, yip, yip, aooooeee" of "Wile E." and his friends. Believe me, if their howls constituted some form of intelligent communication, they weren't plotting how to snare that fast bird with a beeper. They were probably saying, "Let's meet at the hen house."

Actually, while wolves hunt in packs, a coyote is almost always found alone. His predatory strategy is stealth and speed. He lives by the creed of the quick and the dead: if you're not quick, you're dead. He also prefers to avoid any threat to his welfare by going for the easy stuff. A protective mother cow makes a newborn calf a lot less tempting than a fat hen asleep on her roost. In West Texas, the "fox in the hen house" is probably a coyote.

If Smokey and the other dogs who accompanied their masters to the Needmore cotton gin did much talking, some old mutt had probably warned him, "Son, one dog usually don't fare too well against one coyote.

Leave them varmints alone. They just ain't got a sense of humor."

Smokey got the point. When the howling broke loose, he went south. This meant that the drive-through window at the hen house was open for business. More than once, the deacon came close to cussing when his sleep was disturbed by frantic squawks and flapping wings. A barnyard full of feathers would drive him into a rage that further cemented his hatred of varmints.

It was just such a night that caused the farmer's son to miss the school bus. He finally rushed into his home room just before noon. "Lewis, where in the world have you been?" asked his amazed teacher.

"Well, ma'am, 'bout two this mornin', there was a awful racket out in tha barnyard. Pa grabbed his shotgun an' took off outside in jest his slippers and nightgown. It was real dark, and he tried ta sneak up on tha varmint that's been killin' our chickens. He was standin' in tha hen house door with his finger on tha trigger. Old Smokey had followed him, and came up behind him just as he bent over."

"Lewis, that's all very interesting; but what does it have to do with your being half-a-day late for school?" the teacher asked.

Lewis explained: "Well, ma'am, Smokey stuck his cold nose right in the bend of one of Pa's knees and, well, you see, ma'am, we've been cleanin' chickens since 2:30 this mornin'."

Keep It Under Your Hat

"DOES A MAN WEAR A HAT?" WHEN I WAS A boy, that question would have seemed as foolish as asking, "Does a man wear pants?" Every man I knew wore a hat. You could tell a lot about a man just by observing his hat. Englishmen wore bowlers; Frenchmen wore berets; Mexicans wore sombreros; a Turk wore a fez. Cowboys wore ten-gallon Stetsons, a name that described a particular article of clothing in the West as surely as did Levi's® or Justin®. Of course, Roy Rogers and the Lone Ranger taught us that good guys wear white hats, and bad guys wear black hats. Obviously, some of today's singing cowboys don't know that.

My maternal grandfather, who had been a working cowboy before he became a bi-vocational carpenter/preacher, preferred big, broad-brimmed hats. These not only matched up with his tall frame and boots, but also served the practical purposes of shielding off sun and shedding rain. In winter, he wore a gray fur felt with a rolled brim. Summer always called for a new straw hat. When I arrived for my annual summer vacation visit, he immediately took me to town to buy the straw hat that I was expected to wear any time I ventured outside. I would have been ashamed to be seen without it.

When I recall the sights, sounds and smells filed in the deep recesses of my memory bank, two concern my grandfather's hats. The first is the smell of the sweat-soaked straw when he came in to wash up for supper. He would hang his hat on the rack in a corner of the kitchen and splash his face with cold water. As I watched him comb his wet hair, I would think that he looked smaller and exposed without his hat. As I would take it down and try it on, I would remember again how big he was and how far I had to go.

My strongest memory of my grandfather's hat has to do with his habit of taking a brief nap before going back to work after lunch on a hot summer day. He would go out onto the screened-in porch, lie down on the bare wood floor, place his hat over his face and immediately go to sleep. I always wondered why he put the hat over his face until I was lying on a cot in a tent in Africa on a hot afternoon. Flies were interrupting my attempt to rest. In desperation, I covered my face with my hat. It worked, and as I drifted into a pest-free sleep, I muttered, "Now I know."

My father had one hat. It served him well for all occasions, summer and winter, work, play or church. If he was outdoors, he had his hat on. The fact that he was bald had as much to do with this as did the fashion of the day. On one occasion, a customer in Daddy's barber shop asked if he had something to grow hair. Facing the miracle seeker, he replied, "If I said I did, you could take one look and know that I was lying."

"Sharp" is the word for my father's hat. In the tradition of Dick Tracy in pursuit of Prune Face, and Humphrey Bogart in *The Maltese Falcon*, his was a fedora with a snapped brim. He wore it smartly cocked to the left side of his head. To this day, when I hear someone say "handsome," I remember an old snapshot of my parents when they were dating. Recalling how Daddy looked wearing his hat, I still wish that I could look like that.

By the time I became a man, John F. Kennedy and his clan had banished hats from the heads of American males. I felt deeply robbed of a much-anticipated part of manhood.

Now I wear a hat. In fact, I have three. All of them were made in Australia. One, for walking, biking and outdoor work purposes, is called a "Snowy River." Like those worn by the Down Under horsemen of the popular movie, mine is made for the all-weather service valued by my grandfather. Another, called a "Squatter," is for international travel and everyday wear at home. It's a classic open crown that I've given a center crease and a snap brim. This was one of the best Father's Day presents I have received. It has closed a missing link.

Now, I've added one called "The Sydney." It's a true fedora and meets my need for a good dress-up hat. It's the closest I've found to Daddy's classic lid. My hats represent some of the best memories I have of the two best men in my past.

When I must endure the amazed comments of bareheaded friends, I feel awkwardly compelled to explain why I'm wearing a hat. I usually fall back on saying that my doctor has suggested it as one of the best guards against skin cancer. Kindly, I refrain from saying, "If you were smart, you would get one."

If I said what I'm thinking, I would reply, "I'm doing exactly what I've always wanted to do. I'm only sorry it took me 38 years to get around to it. Part of being a man is wearing a hat." More and more, I'm stopped in airports, stores and on the street by someone who says, "I like your hat. Where can I get one like that?" Maybe we are turning a corner and heading in the right direction.

Of course, the influence of a hat can be taken to ridiculous extremes. I heard about a West Texas boy who was the last-born of 15 children. When he arrived, his parents had exhausted their resourcefulness in naming their brood. In desperation, they invited all the neighbors over, explained their dilemma and asked everyone to write a suggested name on a little

piece of paper. The entries were dropped into the pro-
lific father's Stetson. The blindfolded mother slowly
drew out her son's name. From that day, he was known
as "Seven and One-half Smith."

Clean as a Whistle

WHEN YOUR FIRST HERO WAS A COWBOY, your heroes will always be cowboys. My maternal grandfather sealed my choices. He came to West Texas as a Missouri farm boy and got a job as a working cowboy. He earned the nickname of "High Pockets" because his pants were always too big, and the galluses he wore pulled his waistband to just below his breastbone. I've always fancied that, with his red handlebar mustache, he must have looked like a character right out of *Lonesome Dove*.

Even though he left ranch life to follow his call to preach, he never stopped thinking and talking like a cowboy. Long summer hours with him fired my imagination with bucking broncs, mean bulls, jangling spurs and wide-brimmed hats. One annual event brought all this to pulsating life, the Texas Cowboy Reunion in Stamford.

Every Fourth of July week found me decked out in boots and a new straw hat. I was the first one up on the day Mama and Dad would load us into their Pontiac coupe and head out early so we wouldn't miss the parade.

After two hours of sheriffs' posses, high school bands, covered wagons and rodeo queens, I could hardly wait for the event that I anticipated even more than the afternoon rodeo, the big chuck wagon feed. This whole affair was organized by area ranches for real cowboys. The rodeo performers were hands on West Texas spreads. It was a celebration of a heritage unique to the American West. A big part of that heritage is food that "sticks to your ribs." The master chefs of this prairie cuisine were a collection of characters with obvious monikers such as Cookie, Sourdough and Cranky. The best of these brought their range kitchens to Stamford for the Reunion, and their vittles were there to be sampled by all who dared. I didn't just dare; I had cultivated gluttony for an entire year.

After Dad forked over what, even by 1940s' standards, was a bargain fee, we were free to graze. Long wooden tables and benches were set up under tents surrounded by chuck wagons from ranches whose brands and origins I had memorized. Huge kettles and pans offered barbequed beef, pinto beans, sliced onions and tomatoes, sourdough biscuits, peach cobbler, iced tea and, Dad's choice, gallon pots of boiled coffee. Over these helpings, I learned the practical meaning of words such as "sop." Later, I understood exactly what he meant when I heard Tennessee Ernie Ford say, "If you ain't soppin', you ain't livin'."

Drawing vicariously on the authenticity of my grandfather and his cronies, I never saw myself as a drugstore cowboy. For this reason, I always looked derisively on the odd collection of folks who dared to show up at a rodeo without boots. Such dudes could often be heard questioning cooks who offered the more exotic menus. For instance, "Are these 'oysters' fresh?"

An urban housewife was impressed with the sparkling cleanness of one chuck wagon's plates and utensils. She asked the cook how he accomplished this under such primitive conditions. "Well, ma'am," he replied. "I learned ya cain't beat Soap and Water."

Obviously satisfied, the lady filled her plate and disappeared into the crowd. The old cook turned to the shady side of the wagon and called, "Here, Soap! Here, Water! Come 'n git it!"

Fast Train to Clovis

I T IS AN AMERICAN TRAGEDY THAT SO FEW OF today's children have an opportunity to experience the romance of railroads. Muleshoe was founded in 1913 when the Pecos and Northern Texas Railway laid tracks across the county, and was named for the nearby Muleshoe Ranch. The town was incorporated in 1926 and became the county seat of Bailey County. My boyhood home was about a block from the railroad tracks. Now, when I flip through my catalog of memories, some of the best ones involve trains.

We did not own a car until I was a teenager, but don't think we were impoverished. It was just that my frugal father put his money into meeting our real needs. In a town where you could see from city limit to city limit, a car wasn't one of those needs. When we needed to leave town, that's what trains were for.

Railroads and Christmas are intertwined in my memory. Daddy would walk us to the depot lugging suitcases packed with more gifts than clothes. Standing on the platform, we would feel the approaching train before we saw it. The arrival was awesome. The giant steam locomotive passed us belching, shuddering, creaking and hissing, going through all the throes of stopping. At last, the mail-car door slid open, porters leaped down from passenger coaches to place metal steps, and the conductor appeared with his watch in hand. When it was time to leave, I never remember hearing, "All aboard!" Instead I can still hear a clear, drawn-out, "'Board!" piercing the air of a cold winter morning.

By clambering to a seat on the right side of our coach, I could see Daddy walking across the highway on his way to the barber shop a block away. Then, with a shudder, a jerk and a rumble, we were on our way to Sweetwater.

Every town along the way fed my wanderlust. I studied their names on the depot sign and stared down their dusty streets. I tried to imagine the lives of their people and pondered how many towns there must be in the world. I wondered if anyone could live long enough to see them all. If it was possible, I wanted to do it.

Those train rides are still fresh in my memory: Sudan, Littlefield, Roundup, Shallowater, Lubbock (the biggest city in my world), Slaton, Roscoe, Snyder and Post. Then we were there: Sweetwater. My maternal grandfather, Uncle Sam King, was waiting to load us into his car for the trip to Hamlin. There was a railroad to Hamlin, but the only train, other than the freights making runs to and from the gypsum mill, was a strange looking little one-car get-up everyone called a doodlebug. I never rode on it. In a way, that made it even better. I didn't lose the mystery.

Everyone who fascinated me rode trains to all the places where I wanted to go. Mostly, I learned this during weekly visits to our movie theater, the Valley. Spies rode night trains across Nazi-occupied Europe. British empire builders traversed India. Western heroes braved robbers and rock slides while thundering across the frontier on iron horses.

Real-life heroes reinforced the bond between railroads and adventure for me. Notre Dame and Johnny Lujack arrived in Dallas on the train for their showdown with Doak Walker and SMU. The Ringling Brothers Circus came to Lubbock on its own special train.

Believe it or not, Babe Ruth came to Muleshoe on a train. Well, really, he just came through Muleshoe, but I was in the right place when someone shouted the news through the barber shop door. I raced the block to the depot in time to see the now sick and tired "Sultan of Swat" stand on the platform of the rear car and wave as his train slid away to the west.

Later, I landed a job using my bicycle to deliver telegrams. The great thing about that was that the Morse code messages clattered in at the depot. I would hang around watching freights roar past and studying the agent as he operated the telegraph machine. I always remembered that Gene Autry was doing that when a curious Will Rogers asked if Autry could play the guitar propped against the wall.

For one would-be traveler, buying a ticket out of Muleshoe proved to be more than he could handle. His intended destination, Clovis, New Mexico, was only 30 miles away, but at the state line, Central Time changes to Mountain Time. Instantly, an hour is gained.

The traveler approached the ticket agent asking, "What time does the next train leave for Clovis?"

"Three o'clock this afternoon."

"And what time does it arrive in Clovis?"

"Two forty-five this afternoon."

As the bewildered inquirer turned to leave, the agent asked, "Don't you want to buy a ticket?"

"No, sir," he said over his shoulder. "But, if it's okay, I'd like to stand about a hundred yards away and watch that thing take off."

Cat Hair and Cake

MY MATERNAL GRANDMOTHER WAS known in her West Texas church-going community as Sister Josie King. We called her Jo Willie or Mama. She cooked three full meals every day. You could count on it. Even after just she and my grandfather ("Dad" to us) were at home, you could show up unexpectedly, and she was ready. Her meals were all made from "scratch." I've always thought that if I could just find out where she got that stuff and start selling it, every woman could be a great cook.

A "must" to top off lunch, which we called dinner, and dinner, which we called supper, was a freshly baked dessert. Mama excelled with light and moist angel food cakes. Her icing for these turned a light sweet into a real diet buster. Late on a summer afternoon, she had just iced one of these specialties and put it in the middle of the dining room table to cool, when Dad called for her to walk to the garden with him to inspect the tomatoes. Neither of them noticed the cat darting into the house as they stepped through the door onto the front porch.

Fifteen minutes later, they walked back to the house talking about whether the cloud bank in the west would bring a nighttime thunderstorm. Mama carried a generous gathering of okra in the fold of her apron. Dad opened the door for her and was stunned by her scream as she stepped inside.

"My cake! Sam, the cat's eating my cake!"

Sure enough, there was the happiest cat in Jones County. Undeterred by Mama's alarm, his tail switched as he lapped her one-of-a-kind icing.

What happened next was really known only to her, Dad and the cat. Mama would never say whether her preacher husband said something he shouldn't have, but the first words out of his mouth got the cat's attention. As he ran into the dining room, the feline flew into the kitchen. The only route of escape was a locked screen door. This didn't keep him from trying to go through it, nor Dad, now armed with a broom, from encouraging him to do so.

As Mama remembered it, my grandfather preached his best sermon on hell while the desperate cake licker made squalling loops up and down the unyielding screen. The broom made solid, whopping connections at the top and bottom of each loop.

Finally, Mama threw herself into the middle of the mayhem screaming, "Sam, stop it! I've already lost a cake. Don't kill the cat and break down the door."

Throughout the next morning, the battered tom-cat watched from the cover of distant weeds while Dad grumbled through the installation of a new screen door. The two of them never again met on friendly ground. Cat hair and cake just don't go together.

Barber Shops and Bulls

M Y HOMETOWN, MULESHOE, TEXAS, IS the county seat of Bailey County. It's a farming and ranching community on what the Spanish explorers called the Llano Estacado, the Staked Plains. The county is at a high altitude, almost 4,000 feet, and flat. On a clear, hot summer day, you can see grain elevators in Friona, 25 miles away.

When someone asks where Muleshoe is, I always say that it is halfway between Baileyboro and Lazbuddie, and is 18 miles from Earth, all of which is true. Those who have been there will always remember two things, the name and the wind. The wind blows hard most of the time, and everyone develops the habit of leaning into it as they walk. One day the wind didn't blow, and everybody in town fell down.

In 1937, when I was one year old, my father saw an ad in the *Fort Worth Star-Telegram* promising that Lud Taylor in Muleshoe would guarantee a barber $18 a week. To a young man who grew up during the Great Depression on a dryland Jones County farm, that sounded pretty good, so we packed up and moved from Olney to Muleshoe.

For the next 30 years, Daddy gave kids their first haircuts and then stayed around long enough to initiate their kids. For several years, my mother was the only nurse to the only doctor in town. She helped to deliver half of my future classmates.

My first job was shining shoes at the barber shop after school and on Saturdays. Daddy bought the polish, rags and brushes. In return, I swept the floor and kept the cabinets and basins clean. For an 11-year-old, it was a great arrangement. I kept all the money I earned and got the kind of education that comes only from listening to cowboys, farmers, bankers, lawyers, cotton ginners and short-order cooks when there are no women around.

At 20¢ a shine, the money was good, especially on Saturdays. In 1948, Saturday was a big day in Texas county-seat towns. Everybody came early and stayed late. In Muleshoe, the agenda included a double feature at the Valley movie theater, a frosted Coke® at Damron's Drug Store, a week's worth of groceries from Piggly Wiggly, gossip while seated on car fenders in front of St. Clair's Variety Store, a hamburger at Collins Café, a shave and a haircut and a boot or shoe shine. I liked boots because the cowboys tipped best and told the best stories.

One Saturday, as I smoothed polish onto Casey's dress-up boots, he announced, "Man, tha boss almost hung himself this week. Good thang he's got a smart kid."

"What happened?" asked a shave customer from under the hot towel that was softening his whiskers.

"Well, he's never learned the difference in lyin' an' braggin'."

Hearing this really got my attention. I felt that a vital lesson was on the way, since the shop conversations had increasingly confused me about these two things.

"Last Tuesday, I went with him to a horse sale in Clovis, and there was this hotshot from Ruidoso with a race horse. He was tryin' ta con some sucker into bettin' on a stock pony against his high-powered runner.

"I reckon the boss had heard 'bout all his blowin' he could stand. Loud e'nuff fer everbody ta hear, he said, 'Shoot fire, man. I got a bull at my place that can outrun that plug o' yours any day o' tha week.'

"Everbody in tha sales barn laughed it off as a lot of bull, everbody 'cept that New Mexico gambler. He took it for a challenge and said, 'Now, there's a interestin' idy, a bull aginst a horse. How much ya got that says yer beef can race?'

"'If he was here, I'd lay a thousan' on him aginst yer nag right now.' That's what he said, and the place got real quiet. I guess he sensed tha ice gettin' a little thin, 'cause he said, 'But he ain't here, 'n' I'm tired o' listenin' ta you brag. Let's git goin', Casey.'

"I thought that was that 'til th' bettin' man yelled, 'Where's yer place? I'll bring my horse over there!'

"Sure 'nuff, Thursday mornin' we was stackin' hay when I spotted dust on tha road from tha highway. 'Somebody's comin' in a Caddie pullin' a fancy horse trailer,' I said.

"Dumbstruck, tha boss said, 'Blazes, it's that crazy dude with tha race horse. I'm gonna skedaddle. If he comes out here, tell 'im I ain't here.' He took off like a shot cat through a peach orchard and ducked into his back door.

"Tha gambler went straight ta tha house and banged on tha front door. I reckoned the boss had time to sound tha warnin', 'cause his youngest, Ned, went ta tha door 'n' I heard him say, 'Nope, he ain't here. He went to Fort Worth this mornin'.'

"The horse man wasn't gonna be put off that easy. He asked, 'When da you expect 'im back?'

"That's when I thought the kid had blown it, 'cause he said, 'Aw, I reckon he'll be back in time fer supper.'

"That gambler was as flabbergasted as I was by that. He said, 'Why, son, it's more'n 400 miles ta Fort Worth. How'd he go, in a airplane?'

"Just as I was gittin' ready ta cut and run, Ned saved his dad's hide and money. He grinned and said, 'No, sir; he rode that old bull of ours.'"

As Casey handed me two dimes and added a half-dollar, I still wasn't sure about the difference between lying and bragging, but I had concluded that either one usually led to the other.

Fast Thinking

I N THE EARLY '50S, SATURDAYS WERE SPECIAL at the Piggly Wiggly supermarket in Muleshoe. I especially liked the ones during football season. High school football in West Texas is a religion. Most of the games are played on Friday nights, and the only questions on Saturday mornings are "Who won?" and "What was the score?"

Answers to those questions started on the front page of the *Lubbock Avalanche-Journal* and continued in great detail on the sports page. The papers were always tied in a bundle and left in front of the locked doors when everyone arrived early for our 7 a.m. opening. Amazingly, no one was ever late on Saturdays.

Someone with a sharp pocketknife would cut the string and release the papers to eager hands. It was impossible to buy an unused Saturday *AJ* from our store. The crisp autumn air was filled with whoops of joy and groans of despair. An enterprising bread-delivery man would soon arrive to break or make young fortunes, based on the wagers he had booked during the previous week.

Moments later, our red-headed assistant manager would sweep through the crowd of newspaper manglers. After his key turned in the lock, any rare late-comer would be greeted with his raised eyebrow, slight grin and the inevitable question, "Did you have lunch before you came?"

On Saturday mornings, our crew of checkers, stockers, sackers, butchers and produce men took on the focused, high-energy mentality of a battle crew. All over Bailey County, farm and ranch families were getting ready to come to town. Their day would be filled with picture shows, Main Street prize drawings, haircuts, trips to feed stores and lots of talk. At every moment, from early until late, it would be time for someone to buy next week's groceries. After opening, we had two hours at the max to get ready. It was red-alert, all-hands-on-board, man-the-guns, take-no-prisoners, no-horsing-around time.

Until I sacked groceries for the queen mother of a German clan, I didn't believe anyone could buy $100 worth of food at one time. Three married sons and their families all lived in a rural complex with their immigrant parents. Together they farmed five sections of irrigated land. Only the big mama bought groceries, all by herself. We special-ordered her pumpernickel bread and exotic cheeses. (Don't ask me how I managed samples, but today I credit her for many of my strange tastes.) She was our first and best customer every Saturday.

Before noon, the rush was on. By 2 p.m., carts were backed up from the cash registers to the produce racks. This was my finest hour. I took a fierce pride in my speed and efficiency in sacking groceries. It was an art form. Only time and talent could assure knowing when to double bag, never mashing a soft vegetable or breaking an egg, or how to lay a foundation of cans that would exactly fill the bottom of a bag, or when a sack was just full enough to still be lifted by a housewife, and always getting the bread on top.

Sackers were categorized like football players. There were starters, stars, subs and a few who never made the team. Every checker had her favorite, and everybody knew who that was. That allowed for a starting team of three. The second team got in a lot of playing time, because a sacker carried what he had sacked to the customer's car. That meant somebody had to fill the gap. Woe unto the sub who slowed the process, split a sack or squeezed the bread.

Without exception, the guys who embarrassed us the most were the part-timers who were hired for Saturdays only. Generally, they were immature eighth graders and freshmen, known to be incompetent goof-offs. When things heated up, our wrath fell first on them.

Two of these ne'er-do-wells sank to such low levels that I will never be able to forget them or their fates. The piercing scream of the first one stopped everything on the ragged end of a Saturday afternoon rush. His cry had come from a far corner of the back room, from behind the doors that were marked "Employees Only." Little old ladies paled as they looked in that direction. Racing to the rescue, our manager met the Muleshoe Mules' 240-pound tackle and store regular emerging from the presumed disaster area. "What happened?" he asked.

Smiling, but not stopping to elaborate, the hulking athlete replied, "He's in the trash bin."

Only during a saner time, after closing that night, did we all learn what had happened. Our tackle had discovered the goof-off loafing in the back room during a time when all hands were needed. Without a word, he hoisted the diminutive shirker over his head and went straight to the most obnoxious corner of the store, the trash bin. By a Saturday noontime, this catchall reeked with the stench of spoiled lettuce, rotten tomatoes, bad eggs, overripe bananas and things no one wanted to know about. As he was tossed into this unholy mixture, the loafer's scream had stopped traffic in front of the store. He worked hard for the rest of the day, but no closer to other workers than they could help.

One of his tribe's overweight members was found by our produce manager in the fruit and vegetable cooler. The culprit was happily munching on an expensive peach. In a rage, the supervisor slammed the door, dropped a large screwdriver into the lock, flipped the light off from the outside, and went back to work at the front of the store. Things got really busy in a hurry after that. It was an hour later when someone went for fresh tomatoes and found the plump peach eater hugging himself in a corner of the vault. After that, we referred to him as "one of God's frozen people."

A week later, the rescuer of the fruit thief had his own opportunity to gain fame. As he was quietly stripping excess leaves from lettuce and arranging the heads for display, a woman, who had been squeezing oranges, said, "Young man, I want half a head of that lettuce."

Perplexed, he said, "I'll be right back," and went off seeking his manager.

"There's this crazy woman over there who wants to buy half a head of lettuce," he said.

Responding to the strange look on his boss's face, the clerk turned to discover that the customer had followed and was standing directly behind him. Without missing a beat, he smoothly added, "And this wonderful lady wants the other half."

When the satisfied woman had continued on her way, the manager said, "Son, that was quick thinking. I like that in someone who works for me. Did you grow up in Muleshoe?"

"No, sir; I'm from Sudan, the town where they have the best football players and the ugliest women in the world."

"Hey!" reacted the boss. "My wife is from Sudan."

Again, the fast thinker was equal to the challenge. "Oh, really?" he responded. "What position did she play?"

A Shot in the Dark

I N THE 1940S, NO ONE IN MULESHOE HAD EVEN
dreamed of Little League baseball, but every kid
played the game. That was the great thing about
it; everybody played, even girls, if they were so inclined,
and some were very inclined. Everybody had a glove,
almost everybody had a ball and the envied few had a
Louisville Slugger®.

Our diamonds were vacant lots. These varied in
topography. Some were covered with grass burrs and
goat heads; others were barren and hard. None had a
backstop or a center field fence. A home run resulted
from hitting the ball so far that the kid out there
couldn't chase it down, dig it out of the weeds and
throw it back before you crossed the plate. Occasionally, a third-inning homer proved a sudden game winner. When the only ball was hopelessly lost, the game
was over.

From April until October, baseball brought pure joy to my life. It gave birth to fantasies, introduced me to heroes, expanded my world and filled hot afternoons and nights with fierce enjoyment. Its nuances and strategies were dissected in my father's barber shop. Statistics from *The Sporting News* were memorized by my best friend, Billy Ellis, and spoon-fed to me. The voices of Bill Stern and Red Barber made places like Ebetts Field in Brooklyn shrines and men like Bob Feller and Joe DiMaggio icons.

Shining shoes in Daddy's barber shop gave me the privilege of seeing and touching a few men who had been to places and done things I could only dream about. Their names were Moore, and they were my father's regular customers.

Wilcy Moore had played for the Yankees. Daddy granted him special grace. (There were three things my father may not have been able to forgive me for doing: joining the Church of Christ, voting Republican and cheering for the Yankees. In all of my life, I have done only one of those things.) I remember Wilcy as a quiet, strong, still-robust man with an air of confidence that set him apart when he entered the shop. As I shined his shoes, I tried to imagine where those feet had stood.

He had two nephews who carried the hope of following in his steps, and we all hoped for them. Don was a Class A catcher, but that was the end of the road for him. We all believed that his younger brother,

Wilcy's namesake, would have made it to the big time, but his collision with a center field fence in Portland, Oregon, dashed his hopes. I will always remember them because they were the first people I knew who chased their dreams beyond the county line.

"If St. Louis ever gets into the World Series, we will go," promised my father. He said that because, in those days, St. Louis was the closest major league city to Muleshoe. I would read the box scores and study the standings every day and think, "Fat chance!"

While getting to see a real, live major league game seemed beyond hope, professional baseball was close enough for almost any kid to touch during those post-war years. The Class A West Texas-New Mexico League was my connection. There were the Lubbock Hubbers, the Amarillo Gold Sox, the Pampa Oilers, the Borger Drillers, the Abilene Blue Sox, the Albuquerque Dukes and the Clovis Pioneers. Our team was the Pioneers; they played just thirty miles away.

When we couldn't go, we listened to Don Boles broadcast the games over KICA. Daddy taught me to keep box scores. Immediately after supper on game nights, I designed a score card and was in place to pencil in the starting lineup for each team. From that moment, I hung on every play, second-guessing managers, trying to create rallies by the sheer force of will, groaning at errors and experiencing the euphoria of a last-of-the-ninth home run or game-winning strikeout. I expanded my vocabulary with terms such as "Texas leaguer" and "tall can of corn." Often, long after the lights were out, the radios in my bedroom and beside my parents' bed, still told the spellbinding stories of extra innings.

Of course, these broadcasts were pale substitutes for the real thing. The best nights of the summer were spent on the first-base line at Bell Park in Clovis with Daddy and his best friend, Guy Nickels.

Guy was a one-armed cotton ginner. There were a lot of those in Texas during those days. The danger of the cotton conveyer belts was rehearsed in barber shop stories that made me wince. Guy's story was heroic. Alone when the accident occurred, he drove himself to the hospital. Needless to say, I looked upon him with considerable awe. I also looked upon him with boundless gratitude. Our family didn't own a car until I was a sophomore in high school, but Guy never went to a Pioneer game without inviting Daddy and me to accompany him. I can still savor the anticipation I felt on those late-afternoon drives. I can vividly remember my wide-awake late-night attention to the play-by-play rehashing on the return trips.

Getting to a game early was important. There had to be time to watch the warmups, fill in the starting lineup as it was confirmed by the public address announcer, and join everyone in singing "Three Blind Mice" as the umpires marched onto the field. When I had a sack of peanuts in hand, it was game time. I never got over the amazement that the peanuts, or "goobers" as Daddy called them, were salty but still in the shell. I always wondered, "How do they do that?"

Some of the names on the Pioneer roster are still fresh in my mind, like Jess Jacinto at shortstop, Frank Benetes catching and Red Dial pitching. We were there when Dial struck out thirteen men in one game.

Dean was the biggest name connected with the Pioneers. Paul, of the famous Paul (Daffy) and Dizzy Dean brothers pitching team, bought and managed the club. Dizzy visited the park twice when we were there. This sent Daddy and Guy into a frenzy of stories about the brothers. These always included the one about the woman who wrote to Dizzy after he started doing play-by-play broadcasts of baseball. She scolded him for saying "ain't." His reply was, "Ma'am, I know a lot of folks that don't say 'ain't,' but they ain't eatin' as well as I am."

Those night games also prompted stories about the good old days before lighted ballparks. My favorite one had two teams playing far into the fading twilight. It was obvious to everyone that the umpire would call the game because of darkness as soon as the batting team was out. The fielding team held a one-run lead, which would stand for a win if they could survive the current batter. A runner was perched on third base; there were two outs and the count was three balls and two strikes. Every pitch was a shot in the dark. Seizing the moment, the catcher called time-out and strolled to the mound.

"Listen, we can end this thing right now. Give me the ball; I'll hide it in my mitt. You go through the motions; I'll slap my glove and pull the ball out in the strike zone. The ump will never know you threw air, and we'll be outta here."

Moments later the result of the charade was a reverberating, "Strike three! You're out!"

"You're blind as a bat," screamed the outraged batter. "That was a mile high!"

Don't Forget

NOW THAT I'M INTO MY SEVENTH DECADE, I'm more convinced every day that my eyes and my memory have the same control system. I can see things that are far off without much difficulty; but take away my glasses, and I don't have a clue as to what is right in front of me. Equally, the events of my childhood have taken on a new vividness while I dare not go to the store without a list.

Some time ago, on a cold winter night, I turned off the television, picked up a yellow legal pad and started writing down my clearest memories of pre-college days. I was startled as the list quickly soared past 200. These included the smell of cotton gins on a crisp autumn day in Muleshoe, the taste of Bermuda grass sprigs being nibbled under a shade tree, scissor-tailed birds fighting on a late summer afternoon, a baby horned toad in a penny match box, Sunday funny papers and the smell of bacon frying, Gene Autry singing "Rudolph, the Red-Nosed Reindeer," sneaking out of class to listen to the World Series on a pickup's radio, Fibber McGee and Molly, blue suede shoes, school turning out for a special matinee showing of *Lassie Come Home,* and my next-door friend's father coming home from World War II.

Now, where in the world was I last Thursday? I understand that three things go first as one gets older, the memory and...I can't remember the other two. I can identify with the fellow who said, "I couldn't remember anything until I took that Sam Cronigie course."

Even worse was the guy who took a memory course and bragged to a visiting friend about how great it was. "It has literally changed my life," he crowed. "It's the best thing that ever happened to me."

"Boy, I need that," confessed his friend. "What's the name of the course?"

After a long, telling pause, the dumbfounded host asked, "What's the name of that flower that is usually red, and has a long stem with lots of thorns?"

"That's a rose," replied the guest.

"Yeah! Thanks," he stammered. Then he shouted into the kitchen, "Rose, what was the name of that course I took?"

That's bad, but the topper may be the story of the three aging sisters who lived together. The oldest said, "I'm going upstairs to take a bath." A few minutes later she hollered down, "Someone left the tub full of water. Do you want me to drain it?"

"I must have done that," said the middle sibling. "I'll come up and take care of it."

Halfway up the stairs, she paused and called back, "Was I going up or coming down?"

Exasperated, the youngest sister rapped her knuckles on a door frame and mumbled, "Those biddies can't remember anything. I'll knock on wood and be thankful that I'm not like them."

Startled, she asked, "Was that the front door or the back?"

Wildcats, Hornets and Glory

D URING THE 1950S, AN OCTOBER FRIDAY night in a West Texas town had an electric atmosphere and universal significance impossible to describe. A carefully orchestrated series of events built anticipation to the point of explosion. A morning pep rally whipped the high school student body into a frenzy. The crew at the local florist shop kicked into overdrive, cranking out chrysanthemum corsages bedecked in school colors. The driver of a bread-delivery truck booked bets in every grocery store between Lubbock and Muleshoe. By six o'clock, Main Street was deserted and a blaze of lights could be seen on the edge of town. Folks would silently watch an out-of-town school bus make its way toward those lights. In less than two hours, it would be kick-off time.

In towns throughout the Panhandle, across the South Plains and below the Caprock, the explosions were simultaneous. Brass horns blared, drums rolled, cheerleaders pranced and teenage heroes streamed onto brightly lighted fields. Moments later they clashed with the enemy and did battle as Wildcats, Hornets, Mules, Lobos, Eagles, Golden Sandstorms and Westerners. The night would end in glory or despair, not just for the teams and their schools, but for whole communities.

High school football was a rite of passage into manhood for thousands of West Texas schoolboys. Some played because they were natural athletes and had a real zest for combat. For others, the reasons were more complicated: the pressure of a father who would become the grandfather of Little Leaguers, the determination to live up to the exploits of an older brother, a quest for the attention of a cheerleader or a compulsion to prove something to himself. For better or worse, it had to be done. If the team had a winning season, there was glory for all. If not, everyone had ten months to fix blame and anticipate the next campaign.

In Muleshoe, winning seasons were few and far between, but hope was renewed with the approach of each school year. There was the willingness to try anything, short of burnt sacrifices, to turn the corner toward gridiron success. This extended to changing the school colors from gold and purple to black and white, and the team nickname from Yellow Jackets to the Mules. That move put the young players under an additional burden. It doesn't take much imagination to guess the mockery opposing teams made of that name. It was like being a boy named "Sue"—get tough or else.

For any young Texan who put on the armor of a Friday-night warrior, some things are impossible to forget: grass burrs and festered knees, cheeks below the eyes blackened with soot from the tailpipe of a school bus, the taste of blood from one's own nose and the jar of being dashed to a hard caliche surface.

If pressed to recall the most remarkable football games of my teen years, three come immediately to mind. For the rush of sheer euphoria, it would have to be the night Muleshoe defeated Sudan for the first time in 15 years. The fire whistle blew, car horns honked until midnight and every play was replayed for a week.

For blood, guts and glory, it would have to be the November battle for the regional championship between six-man teams from Lazbuddie and Darouzett. Played on a rock-hard field, the entire event was a storm of grunts, cracks and groans.

For the drama of the passing of an era, it had to be the defeat of Abilene by Highland Park in the Cotton Bowl for the Texas State Championship. At the end of regulation time the score was tied; the Scotties finally won on penetrations.

Winning was the objective. The routes attempted were many and varied. It was amazing how many outstanding players' fathers found really good jobs in oil field towns. It was said that these schools had the best teams money could buy.

Pity the coach who failed to produce a winner, whatever the quality of the material he was given to work with. One poor soul discovered just how dire the consequences could be. To say he was fired doesn't begin to tell the story. The school board vowed that he would never coach again. In addition, they determined that he would never be able to work again, period. Slowly, the reality of his situation soaked in. He couldn't even hire out to clean stables. He was desperate when the circus came to Amarillo. With hat in hand, he begged the manager for any kind of job.

"Well," the boss said, "We usually carry a full crew, but I might just have something. It is a little unusual and you might consider it demeaning."

"I'll do anything," the humbled coach admitted.

"Don't be too quick," he was warned. "We've had a tiger that has been our strongest draw. Everyone who buys a ticket expects to see him. The problem is that he up and died yesterday."

"So?" asked the coach.

"So," said the circus boss. "We have his skin, head, claws—everything—and, well, I was just thinking that if you would be willing to put all that on and act like a tiger, I'd pay you $15 a day."

Without blinking twice, the coach blurted, "I'll do it!"

That first day, he felt awkward, but he finally managed a growl or two and collected his money. The second day, he got into the swing of things and was a real crowd pleaser. He paced, roared, slashed and menaced.

Suddenly, the door was raised at the end of his cage and a huge lion was released to share his space. In panic, he shook the bars and screamed for help. The lion jerked his tail and said, "Shut up and calm down! You're not the only football coach who's out of work."

Saturday!

SATURDAY! JUST HEARING THE WORD STILL brings back a flood of some of my most vivid childhood memories. Saturdays in the West Texas of the '40s and '50s were very special. They ended the old week with an exclamation mark and assured that the new one would be filled with anticipation. Everyone went to town on Saturday, and the town came alive. In fact, the phrase "Now you're really going to town" was synonymous with great accomplishment.

In towns, Fridays were spent preparing for Saturday. Sale prices were painted on store windows, shelves were stocked and eye-catching displays were built. The day was about to dawn that would make it possible to stay open for another week.

After closing on Friday afternoon, my father lingered in the barber shop long enough to sharpen his shears and razors for the big day. This included one particular razor, which was reserved for two regular

Saturday customers. These grizzled old codgers epitomized what the day was all about. They were bachelor brothers who came to town once a week, on Saturday. That trip unfolded in a ritual that would not vary.

It all began with baths in the shared hot water that had been poured into a number 3 size washtub in the middle of their kitchen floor. I always wondered who took the first bath. It couldn't have been much fun bathing in once-used water, but this was typical of many rural residents in that day and time. Next, they donned their blue, bibbed overalls and long-sleeved khaki shirts, buttoned at the collar. Oiled, high-topped work shoes and white socks completed getting dressed up. Now their goal was to get to town early enough to secure one of the choice parking places on Main Street. (Where one parked was very important. It made all sorts of things possible, such as not having to move the car to load groceries, being able to offer two fenders to the news commentators of the day and being positioned to watch the latest technological marvel, television, in a store window.)

Also, getting to town early gave the brothers a welcome relief from their own sorry cooking. In Muleshoe, the coffee shop next to my father's barber shop and the café at the corner of Main and the Clovis highway offered the best opportunities to eat out before going to the picture show. Gourmet choices ranged from chili and crackers to hamburgers. The heavier selections such as chicken-fried steaks with cream gravy or T-bones and French-fried potatoes waited for those who decided to eat supper in town.

After the noon meal, which we all called dinner, it was time to get in line at the Valley Theater. The full-colored poster, locked behind glass near the ticket window, added to the expectancy. Johnny Mack Brown, Gene Autry, Roy Rogers or Jimmy Wakely waited just beyond the overflowing popcorn machine.

Soon after the movie crowd emerged, squinting and sneezing, into the mid-afternoon sunshine, it was time for the biggest event of the day, the Saturday afternoon drawing. Families had eagerly filled out their entries a week earlier; now fingers were crossed and hope soared.

Farmers and their wives still had strong memories of the Great Depression. A season of drought or a hailed-out crop brought the old fears raging back. Any hedge against hard times was more than welcome. The drawings for money pooled by local merchants offered some hope.

A flatbed trailer would be towed by a tractor to the middle of Main Street an hour before the drawing. Horn-shaped speakers were put in place to amplify the music of a country and western band, the promises of some county politician and, finally, the announcement of the winning number. I'll never forget how impressed and proud I was on the Saturday that my Aunt Ethel was cajoled from her checker's position in a Hamlin, Texas, grocery store to climb up on the trailer and sing "You Are My Sunshine."

With the drawing over, the rush was on to get everything done. For almost every man and boy, this meant a haircut and, for the men, a shave. This brought the dreaded moment for my father. The bachelor farmers had cultivated six days of beard growth that Daddy called "barbed wire." His best razors were placed out of sight, and the one reserved for this weekly challenge was brought forth. I can still hear the sound of it being pulled through the stubble that not even the lather and hot towels could soften. With the task completed, the brothers were ready for Sunday worship and a hard week of isolation in the fields.

As a shoeshine boy in the barber shop, Saturdays were a bonanza for me. Cowboy boots were attacked at 20¢ per pair. A week's accumulation of manure and mud caused me to constantly question my own prices, but generous tips and long hours often netted $20 to $30 in one day. This was an astounding amount of money for a 12-year-old kid in 1948. From that time, I bought my own clothes and always had my own spending money.

After the barber shop, the bachelors' last stop was the grocery store. During high school days, I discovered the horror of Saturday as a "grunt" charged with sacking and carrying out groceries. At 5:00 in the afternoon, every cash register would be ringing, and customers with full carts would be backed up to the farthest wall. The pace would continue unabated until well after 9 p.m. It was a challenge to dexterity, physical strength, mental toughness and nervous stability. With reckless speed, cans, butter, bread, eggs and vegetables had to be mixed in just the right arrangements so that the sacks arrived at homes with everything in its purchased condition. Names of regular customers had to be remembered. We had to just smile when we asked, "Where is your car?" and were told, "Outside."

Out of this chaos, I formed a fantasy that I've never forgotten. As I sweated through a marathon of packing, lifting and rushing, I would spot a guy all dressed up, with freshly shined boots. He would be leaning against the wall drinking a soda pop and eating salted peanuts. I would think that someday I would not have to work on Saturdays. When that day came, I promised myself I would get all dressed up, pay someone to shine my boots, go to the busiest store in town and watch people work. I've never done this, but I still think about it.

My best Saturday memories preceded my twelfth summer. Those earlier years included long stays with my grandparents in their rural Jones County home. This caused "going to town" to take on real meaning. My Nazarene grandfather didn't believe in going to picture shows, but an afternoon perched on a car fender listening to him and a parade of philosophers, political pundits, homespun humorists and world-class liars provided the best entertainment to be had. I still wonder just how much my sense of humor, political leanings and moral attitudes were shaped by what I heard on those afternoons.

Of course, this was back when children were to be seen and not heard. An indulged, spoiled kid was destined to catch more than his share of critical attention. One such brat had an early reputation for exaggeration. Before leaving for town one Saturday morning, his embarrassed father threatened his life. "If you start to stretch the truth today, I'm gonna stretch your neck," he was warned. "If I jerk on your sleeve, straighten your yarn out pronto."

A mid-afternoon lying and bragging session on Main Street proved too much for the little fibber. The conversation turned to barns, big barns. Suddenly, the adult voices were silenced by the boy crowing, "Shucks, y'all shoulda seen tha barn we had 'fore we moved here. Why it was four hunnerd feet tall..." Suddenly, a strong jerk on his right shirt sleeve yanked him back to reality. "And," he concluded, "six feet wide."

Sick and Tired

B
Y THE TIME I WAS TEN YEARS OLD, I WAS sick and tired of being sick and tired. I owed it all to being privileged to grow up in the "good ole days" when everyone ate natural, organic foods, and you could eat meat and drink milk without some chemist having messed with it. We bought raw milk from a wholesome little lady whose cows had not been tested. The down side was that, when I was six years old, I contracted a disease that plagued me with anemia until I was eleven. One day I was in school; the next day I was in bed. That was my domain for the next seven months.

Adapting to those circumstances still marks my life. I learned to be content being alone for long periods of time. I learned to study small details and let them release my imagination. The shape of a stain on wallpaper took on bizarre significance. The progress of an insect on a window sill became a real event.

I learned to savor sights and tastes, especially tastes. Today, when I remember two of these tastes, it is as though I have them in my mouth: Hershey's® bars—they're good—and iron tonic—that's not good. I slowly ate a Hershey's® bar every afternoon, breaking the squares off one at a time and letting each piece melt in my mouth. Now, I'm a chocoholic beyond hope.

Radio was my gateway to the larger world. Every day I'm thankful for a childhood before television. If I'd had access to a steady diet of game shows, sleaze talk shows and soap operas, my young brain would have turned to mush. Instead, I constantly visited the theater of my mind. Long after the latest episode of The Lone Ranger, Sky King, Jack Armstrong or The Green Hornet, I would lie in the dark and continue to spin out my own extensions of their adventures.

My favorite retreat was a secret room under the house, where I had a special telephone directly connected to the FBI. The agent who was my contact had supplied me with a shortwave radio that put me in touch with the world. Periodically, I would be called on to accompany a male and female agent disguised as their son. Trained in the martial arts and fully armed, I joined them in battling Nazi spies, oriental warlords and western cattle rustlers.

Some of my superheroes became visual from the pages of comic books. When this wasn't possible, I gave them faces, muscular bodies, fast horses, sleek airplanes and cars, plus villains to combat. I did this on any paper I could get my hands on, using pencils, fountain pens and crayons. By the time I was 11, if all my drawings had been saved, my primitive portfolio would have filled a steamer trunk. To this day, I have an overwhelming urge to buy when I see a giant box of Crayolas® at Wal-Mart.

Too often, the fun and games were interrupted with trips to the office of Dr. Dudley, or to the hospital near his office in Clovis, New Mexico. I became a master artist at disassociating while having a blood sample taken or while taking glucose intravenously.

All of this wiped out any tendency that I might have had to be a hypochondriac. I hate the thought of being sick. I war against it. I refuse to entertain any ache, sniffle or nausea. I have taken a vow. Sickness is not welcome. It will have to drag me down kicking and screaming. This is just as well, because my mother gave me all the sympathy of a Marine Corps DI. She loved; she cared; but she was tough. No kid at our house could have ever missed school by feigning a headache or an upset stomach. She was too smart and too mean. We didn't dare.

When my father moved us to Muleshoe in 1937, Mother went to work as the nurse to the only doctor in town. She helped to deliver half the kids with whom I attended school. For the next 17 years, she was a nurse, a teacher of private speech and drama classes, and the operator of the town's first private kindergarten—more food for my already overactive imagination.

Some of the most memorable stuff I have ever heard is from my mother's doctor's office stories. Unfortunately, some of this is the most unrepeatable stuff I have heard.

Most of those West Texas doctors were earthy characters who were on a first-name basis with all their patients. They wisely mixed horse sense with book learning. Their diagnosis may have been deficient in Latin phrasing, but it was on target in practicality. My favorite story is about a doctor diagnosing an ailing cowboy. The old doctor asked, "Son, have you ever had this before?"

"Yep," answered the patient.

"Well, I reckon you've got it again," said the doctor.

Sometimes their prescribed remedies were more than a little unorthodox. This was discovered by a farmer who brought his wife to the doctor because she had "come down with the blues." After a brief chat with the depressed woman, the physician called the worried husband into his office. Without warning, he took the startled wife into his arms and kissed her. Turning to the farmer, he insisted, "Your wife needs that every day."

Scratching his head, the husband said, "Doc, I can get her in here a couple of times a week, but I sure don't know about every day."

Boys Will Be Boys

T O BE A BOY DURING THE '40S AND '50S WAS to enjoy a safer time of innocence and stability. Then, the boundaries were clearly marked, and the consequences for transgression were sure and swift. Still, the challenge of testing them was irresistible, and the enforcers were reliable and loving. Now the lines are blurred, and the consequences uncertain but potentially deadly.

Our Gang, of movie fame, had its counterparts in every community: girl-avoiding, imaginative, self-assured, adventure-seeking tykes whose families made up a cross section of society. In a single day, their minds and hands could produce the bizarre, gross, startling and exasperating, but no one's life was ruined and no mother's heart was broken.

Two nine-year-olds strolling down a Main Street sidewalk would provoke predictable comments from barber shop regulars familiar with their reputations:

"Here comes trouble looking for a place to happen."

"If those kids had dynamite for brains, they wouldn't have enough between them to blow one nose."

"Yeah, but boys will be boys."

"Kids today ain't as tough as we were. Nowadays, they chunk dirt clods at each other. In our day we used corn cobs that had soaked for a week. Them things would raise a welt that would stay with you for a month of Sundays."

Clod fights were the sure result of seeing the latest hand-grenade-tossing war flick. Days would be devoted to digging trenches and building forts. A wise father knew better than to take a short cut across a vacant lot on a dark night. There was no telling what might be new there since his last stroll. Future pitchers and quarterbacks went first when the sides were chosen for clod fights. The rules were simple: if you got hit, you were dead. When the right guy threw an apricot-sized piece of caliche and caught you in the middle of the back, no one had to tell you that you were dead. Most battles ended in surrender to superior talent long before the casualties became massive.

Every victorious army must award medals, and we had ours. Before anyone heard of pop-top aluminum cans, soda pops came in a vast array of bottle styles and cap color. The caps from Nu-Grape®, Royal Crown Cola®, Big Red®, Orange Crush®, Dr. Pepper®, Delaware Punch® and Coca-Cola® made perfect battle decorations. The first trick was to get the cork inside the cap out in one piece. This was then pressed, from inside your shirt, back into the cap, on the outside of your shirt. After taking three or four enemy forts in one day, a guy's shirt would be covered with pop caps. The second trick was for him to keep his mother from killing him when she picked up his dirty clothes that night.

Battlefield communications were made possible by punching a hole into the bottom of a bean can with a rusty nail. Twine was pushed through from the outside and knotted on the inside. Two cans were secured at opposite ends of a long strand of string. When it was tightly stretched from one camouflaged site to another, the sound transmission was surprising.

Of course, all soldiers need "R & R," so equal gusto was devoted to projects designed to produce pure pleasure. Some test of skill or courage was still built in, just to make sure everyone kept his competitive edge. The most memorable device came into being when two brothers, half a block away, got hold of the longest and thickest piece of rope any one of us had ever seen. After several knots had been tied at various lengths from one end, the other end was tied to a strong, high branch of a huge tree in the middle of their backyard.

A shed opposite the tree made a perfect launching place for a multitude of egged-on daredevils. The rush of swooping across the yard, like Errol Flynn coming to the rescue of Olivia de Havilland, was unbeliev-

able. That soon lost its edge, however, and the ultimate challenge was to let go of the rope at exactly the
right moment so that you landed farther from the take-
off point than the last clown who had flung himself
thrashing and screaming into space. Miraculously, the
broken arm or neck, predicted by every mother in town,
never materialized.

Every now and then, a few of us did walk on the
edge. This was usually not maliciously plotted, but
provoked by unexpected opportunity and circumstance. This occurred late one summer afternoon,
when a friend from down the street showed up with
an almost exhausted spool of copper wire. "Isn't it
neat?" he asked.

"Yeah," I agreed. "Where did you get it?"

"A repair guy, who's been working at our place,
left it. What should we do with it?"

"I know," I said, remembering a scene from a re-
cent cowboy movie. The bad guys had stretched a rope,
from tree to tree, across a mountain trail. That night,
when unsuspecting cowboys rode past, they were
swept from their saddles. I knew we couldn't anticipate any passersby on horseback. Besides, that scenario carried a high probability of somebody getting
hurt. The plan I was hatching was designed to answer
the question "What would happen if...?"

"Let's tie one end to this tree here and tie the other
end to that tree over there," I suggested, pointing to
the opposite side of the street.

"Wow! What do you think will happen?"

Playing it out in my mind, I said, "I think, if we get it right at bumper height, it will snap in the middle with a terrific 'whack.' They'll never know what happened."

Bad idea and bad plan! The wire wasn't quite bumper high; it missed by about an inch. Instead, the wire met the front tires of a passing Buick, snapped at each extremity and whipped around the car's wheels with a "whang," "whirr" and "zap, zap, zap" louder than anything we could have imagined.

Our worlds, for that day, came to an end when the neighbor, who had been watching the whole thing, stepped onto his porch and told us to stay put. Moments later, our fathers came striding across from our yards. As I said, in those days, consequences were sure and swift.

It is true that as our corps of kids progressed into adolescence, the pranks acquired a broader scope, and there was a greater necessity for anonymity. Some things just happened.

Apparently, no one in the entire county had any idea who the culprits might be. In spite of this, occasionally you would hear someone relate the happening and supply details that had not been previously published. For instance, the presence of the "high school cats" was traced back to two freshmen who were joyriding along a county road on a Sunday afternoon. Attracted by a squirming burlap bag in the ditch, they discovered a batch of discarded kittens. Later, the bag's contents were emptied through a barely open class-room window. Two years later, wild-eyed felines still could be found in unexpected campus locations.

Halloween brought the nights when legends were born. The mornings after always found cotton trailers parked in the middle of Main Street intersections and store windows decorated with paraffin.

Each year, one or two pranks topped the charts and dominated bridge party and barber shop conver-sations for weeks afterward. The most daring may have been the small paper sack of chicken droppings that was set afire on the porch of a high school teacher. The vocabulary that rained down on the neighborhood, as he stomped out the blaze, had never been heard in his classroom.

Indoor plumbing had not found its way into every 1940s home. Outhouses, bordering alleys, were still a common sight. These were prime targets for bands of marauding spooks. Those who toppled them were threatened with things too terrible to mention. Woe unto the poor soul who was identified among the guilty!

An otherwise decent and honest young man found himself being confronted by his angry father on the morning after Halloween. "Were you with those hood-lums who turned over our toilet last night?"

Gulping, the boy answered, "Father, I cannot tell a lie. Yes, I did it."

Enraged, the father said, "I'm going to give you the whipping of your life."

"But, Dad," the boy protested. "George Washington told the truth about cutting down the cherry tree and his father didn't spank him."

"Yes," his father said. "But George Washington's father was not in the cherry tree!"

A Funny Thing
Happened at Church

I F GOD DOESN'T HAVE A SENSE OF HUMOR, why do so many funny things happen when people go to church? No sacred thing seems to be off limits for hilarious faux pas and pratfalls in pews or behind pulpits.

Going to church was never an option for my brother and me. Our maternal grandfather was a bi-vocational Nazarene preacher, and our father was the son of a Baptist deacon. I was probably ten years old before I knew there were people who didn't go to church.

Of course, when I started to school, it didn't take long to discover that not all of my classmates went to the same church. In Muleshoe, there were a lot of Baptists, at least three different kinds. I had a cousin whose group really fascinated me. They had church only once a month, but they made up for lost time by preaching all day and washing each other's feet. Compared to them, our bunch at First Baptist was pretty bland.

It seemed that the biggest part of my classmates who weren't Baptists were members of the Church of Christ. I was always amazed that their music sounded as good as ours, and they didn't even have a piano. I was also jealous because they got grape juice every Sunday. Methodists may not have had the numbers, but they had the class: the classiest weddings, the classiest windows and the classiest girls.

As a boy, I was never sure I had sorted out all the differences in the various churches. My favorite haunt, my father's barber shop, was not always the best place to get a theological education, especially if you were already a candidate for a chapter in "Gullible's Travels."

During a prolonged summer drought, a dryland cotton farmer came into the shop beating dust off his hat. "I declare," he said. "It's so dry that I hear the folks over at the Church of Christ are sprinkling, the Baptists are using a wet wash rag and the Methodists are giving rain checks."

Because my grandfather, whom I greatly admired, preached in Churches of the Nazarene, my Baptist loyalty was sorely tested during long summer vacations with him and my grandmother. During worship, they sang "I stand amazed in the presence of Jesus the Nazarene." I would think, "John was a Baptist, but

Jesus was a Nazarene. Am I sure I'm playing for the right team?"

Getting up on Saturday and Sunday mornings was not a problem for me. Saturday was an adventure, and I didn't dare waste a minute. Sunday had colored funny papers and the best breakfast of the week going for it. While pancakes or waffles, bacon and eggs and strong coffee were filling the house with their enticing aromas, my brother and I flanked Daddy on the living room couch. He held the funny papers, and we all followed along as a guy on KGNC in Amarillo read them over the radio. This all took place in plenty of time for us to study our Sunday School lessons.

My memories of Sunday School in Muleshoe are tied forever with the name of Byron Griffiths. He and his wife, Truma, had no children of their own, but they invested huge chunks of their lives in quite a batch of us brats. I know that Mr. Griffiths taught some great Sunday School lessons, but that's not what I really remember. I remember him for initiating one of the greatest mysteries of my childhood. Ours was a very democratic class. We voted on everything: whether to have a class picnic, about exchanging gifts at Christmas, class officers—you name it. Our teacher would always say, "Everyone in favor, lift a hand." Then, I thought I would hear him say, "Everyone opposed, vote by a black sign."

This baffled me. I didn't know what the black sign was. I thought that this must have been explained on a Sunday when I was not present. I was never against anything, but it troubled me that I would not know what to do if I was. I wasn't about to let everyone know what a dummy I was by asking for clarification. Instead, I determined to keep my eyes and ears open and try to solve the mystery.

My first tactic was to raise issues that required a vote, hoping that someone would be opposed. This was fruitless. We were a class of lemmings. No one would break with the pack. This crowd would have voted unanimously to go swimming at the North Pole. Weekly, my bewilderment deepened. Thinking about it kept me awake at night and made efforts to concentrate on school work futile. Almost every moment was devoted to trying to find out how to make a "black sign."

Finally, I swallowed my pride and waited one Sunday until everyone had left the classroom, then I blurted out, "Mr. Griffiths, how do you make the 'black sign'?"

I was incredulous when he replied, "I don't know."

"Well, great," I thought. "How does he expect anyone else to know if he doesn't?"

"What are you talking about?" he asked.

"You know, when we're voting, you say, 'Everyone opposed vote by a black sign.'"

What he said next, I heard clear as a bell and I understood every word. "I don't say 'black sign.' I say, 'Vote by a like sign.'"

So much time and energy had been devoted to solving the great black sign mystery that there was a big hole in my life for weeks after that anticlimactic Sunday.

Slowly, my barber shop education caused me to realize that there were pagans among us, people who went to dances, patronized bootleggers and skipped Sunday School. I also became convinced that God's best protection against this waywardness was a mother who could get and keep your attention.

At the laundry on a Monday morning, one such mom talked about her most trying Sunday morning. "I had called that boy three times already," she said. "Finally, I jerked his bed covers off and yelled, 'Fred, get up right now. You're going to be late for church.'

"He bowed his back, put his pillow over his head and mumbled, 'I'm not going to church today.'

"Well," she said. "I jerked the pillow away and said, 'Oh, yes, you are!'

"'No, I'm not,' he insisted. 'I don't like the people there and they don't like me, so tell me why I should go.'

"I yanked that pillow away again and reminded him, 'You're going because you are 45 years old and the pastor of the church.'"

That's not hard to understand when I think back on the disruptions that plagued our pastor's preaching. There was this one kid who was always parked on the second pew in the center section. To the preacher, he must have looked like an infantile gargoyle. His surprise antics had been hurled like grenades in mid-sermon so many times that the pastor developed a twitch.

One Sunday, the preacher dramatically asked a packed house, "Who are the redeemed of the Lord?"

"I don't know!" shouted the intent boy. His embarrassed mother drove a sharp elbow into his rib cage. Groaning, he protested, "But I don't know!"

Complicating this child's good conduct record at church was a chronic bladder problem. He went before, during and after, especially during. Answering the call of nature at a revival meeting service, he endeared himself to the visiting evangelist by traipsing up the aisle, turning at the back door to face the platform and announcing loudly, "I'm going to the bathroom."

Laughter had just subsided and order had been restored, when the preacher suddenly stopped in mid-sentence and stared at the back of the auditorium. Slowly people turned to see what was happening. The young menace was standing in the doorway, as if waiting to be recognized. At just the right moment, when he had everyone's attention, he said, "The lights are out and it's dark in there."

Our pastor almost had a nervous breakdown on the Sunday morning when not one, but two, small boys graced the up-front pew. Apparently, he was reassured and able to continue because one was his visiting grandson. This boy, however, created his own commotion by constantly asking his grandmother questions.

When the ushers walked forward carrying wooden plates, he stage-whispered, "What's happening?"

"They are going to receive the offering," he was told.

Moments later, the pastor motioned for the congregation to stand. "What does that mean?" the boy asked.

"It means that we're going to stand and sing the doxology."

When it was time for the sermon, the pastor's grandson was fascinated to see his grandfather remove his wristwatch and place it on the pulpit. Tugging at his grandmother's sleeve, he asked, "What does it mean when Papa does that?"

Smiling down at him, the pastor's wife replied, "It doesn't mean a thing."

All Night Jazz and the Baptist Hymnal

F OR A GUY WHO IS TONE DEAF AND CAN'T carry a tune, music has always been as much a part of my daily routine as food. It was predictable; it's in my genes. Our family would beg my father not to embarrass us by singing in church, but by the time I was ten, I had heard him sing Jimmy Rogers' songs until I knew them by heart. While in the shower, I still break into "T's for Texas" and scare my dog by trying to yodel.

Victrola record players, radios and Wurlitzer Jukeboxes were the '40s and '50s forerunners of today's boom boxes, tape decks, CD players and Walkmans®. My aunt Ethel owned a record player and had a lot of 78 rpm records to go with it. During hot summer afternoons, I would spend hours arranging stacks of Ink Spots, Andrews Sisters, Glenn Miller and Bing Crosby platters to create just the right mood.

Radios have been everywhere I have gone. I have made sure of that. My favorite was a Zenith® tabletop model in a plastic cabinet. For all my school years, it was moved back and forth between my desk and my bedside table. It was never out of reach.

Daily doses of Eddy Arnold singing "The Cattle Call" and a weekly Saturday night trip to "The Grand Ole Opry" sowed country music into my psyche so thoroughly that it keeps sprouting like crabgrass. For no socially redeeming purpose, I went through high school singing "Your Cheatin' Heart" and doing weird vocal imitations of a steel guitar playing "Under The Double Eagle." Now, while some adults secretly eat Kellogg's® Frosted Flakes, I am a closet Willie Nelson fan.

It took a good friend, who favored white buck shoes and who had a '41 Ford coupe with a strong truck radio, to bring some sophistication to my tastes. That radio would pull in anything in the air. We would spend nights dragging Main Street in Clovis, New Mexico, or cruising the back roads of Bailey County. During those nocturnal hours, I discovered jazz. Stan Kenton's progressive styling beamed in from the turntables of KVOO atop Tulsa's Phil Tower. The best LP I had ever heard was a blend of Gershwin-style music and narration with thunderstorm and New York night-traffic sound effects. It filled a long segment of American Airlines' "Music Til Dawn," on a 50,000-watt clear channel station from Los Angeles. The record was called "My

Tower." Late Sunday nights were reserved for WWL in New Orleans and Dixieland jazz.

A jukebox at a café on the Clovis highway and KLLL in Lubbock gave me my first jolts of rock 'n roll. What I'm talking about was a far cry from the violent, head-smashing blast of today's rock. This was a thumping, happy blend of what had reverberated from Memphis, the Louisiana bayous and Tennessee hills for years. Instead of finding its themes in drugs and the occult, it settled for girls named Peggy Sue and blue suede shoes. This got tied in with black pants and pink belts, "Mr. B" collars, duck-tail haircuts, iridescent socks and poodle skirts—all the stuff needed to fuel "Happy Days" and *Grease* for another generation.

Church, the training ground for hundreds of musicians and the birthplace for much that has found its way into every style, put a song in my heart sooner than I can remember. What we sang at church on Sunday, we sang all week. My mother sang "In The Garden" while she washed dishes. My father sang "The Old Rugged Cross" while he tied his necktie. My grandfather sang "This World Is Not My Home" while he sharpened saws. Everybody I knew could sing 20 or 30 hymns by memory. While working, driving around or walking to school, you could start "Amazing Grace" or "At The Cross," and two or three buddies would join in.

In contrast to today's churches, where hymnals are removed and hard rock dominates youth sessions,

I don't remember ever going to church expecting to hear an imitation of Bill Haley and the Comets. I don't think anyone in our youth group ever dropped out because the worship service wasn't "with it." We expected church to be different.

Still, hymnbook language was a little hard to master as a child. Until I learned to read, I was baffled every time we sang about "Gladly the cross-eyed bear." I was never sure what I was doing when I raised my "Ebenezer."

All this diversity shaped me into an adult whose favorites include Pavarotti, Emmy Lou Harris, Ramsey Lewis, Steve Green and Carman. I'm sure my greatest capacity for tolerance is in the area of music. Until I've heard it, I withhold judgment, and there is still a lot to hear.

Oscar, the owner of a Muleshoe sheet music store, thought he had heard it all until a prospective customer requested a piece that blew his mind. "We don't have it," he admitted. "I'm sure we can get it for you, though."

Determined to fill the order, he placed a call to the largest music supplier in Dallas, only to get a wrong number. "Do you have Ten Little Fingers and Ten Little Toes in Tennessee?" he asked a startled plumber.

After a long pause, he got his answer. "No, but I've got a wife and eight kids in Texas."

Taken aback, Oscar asked, "Is that a record?"

"No, I don't think so, but it's above average," was the reply.

I Must Be Dreaming

DUST BOWL-PRODUCING WEATHER, DRY-
land cotton crops, low cattle prices, sick kids
and too-vivid memories of the Great Depression brought on a lot of bad dreams for farmers and
ranchers in the West Texas of my childhood. Most of
those got dumped and analyzed in my father's barber
shop.

Local clip joints have always been for more than a
trim and a shave. The barber has historically held out
the hope of therapy. The red and white stripes of the
barber pole symbolized blood and bandages. My father and his contemporaries were never hesitant to
put a Band-Aid® on a troubled mind as well as a nicked
chin.

It would be impossible to count the times I heard
an early-morning shave customer sigh and say, "Boy,
I had the wildest dream last night."

Daddy's "Yeah? Tell me about it," set the agenda for the next 30 minutes.

"I shoulda kept my mouth shut 'bout it," moaned Shorty, as he settled into the chair on a Monday morning. "Now, my wife's ready to kill me."

"Uh-oh!" Daddy exclaimed. "You must've dreamed about another woman."

"Nope," said Shorty. "I dreamed all night that I was eating marshmallows, and now we can't find that newfangled foam rubber pillow the Missus brought home from Clovis."

Some dreams had life-changing potential. I learned this on a Saturday morning when Rick, one of Muleshoe's few really dedicated golfers, showed up at the shop shaken and looking for objective input.

"You don't look too good," observed Daddy. "What's wrong?"

"I dreamed that I died, and it was terrible."

"You mean...?"

"Yeah," confessed Rick. "I ended up out of bounds, in the devil's rough."

"What was it like?" queried Daddy, as half a dozen curious bench warmers leaned forward.

"It was weird, really weird," Rick said. "Here I was with old Lucifer himself on the most beautiful championship course you can imagine. Then he presents me with this customized set of clubs and introduces me to three guys who each shot par every Sunday of their adult lives. Then he says, 'It's all yours. Have fun.'

"Well, I can tell you," said Rick. "I could hardly wait to tee up. I selected a driver, put a tee between my teeth and unzipped the ball pocket of my new bag. 'Hey,' I said. 'I can't find any golf balls.'

"'And you won't either,' said the senior member of my foursome."

No one was surprised when Rick showed up at church the next day. Tragically, that was the morning the pastor dreamed that he was preaching and, when he woke up, he was.

If It's Liver,
It Must Be Wednesday

WHEN I WAS A BOY, WE NEVER HAD TO wonder what time it was or what day it was. The radio took care of the time. If Cotton John was kicking off his early-morning farm show on KGNC in Amarillo by declaring that this was the "best part of the Golden Spread day," it was 5 A.M. and time to hit the floor. If the trials and tribulations of Ma Perkins were filling the kitchen, it was 1 P.M. and time to wash the noon dishes. If Gabriel Heater was intoning, "Ah, there's good news tonight," it was 6 P.M. and time to eat supper.

Days could be determined by the inflexible routines that ruled our lives. If Mother was hauling a load of dirty clothes to the laundry, it was Monday. If my brother and I were being herded to the bathtub, it was Saturday.

Food, however, was the most dependable way of identifying days. Somewhere our mother had seen that written in stone. Shortages and rationing during World War II gave birth to some innovative food concoctions. One of these was our regular Monday "delight," Spam®. Oh, boy, what a blessing!

On Tuesdays, canned salmon was made into patties or croquettes and fried. They were great smothered in catsup. I'll never forget my utter amazement when, as a college student, I journeyed to Portland, Oregon, and saw a thick salmon steak. "Wow!" I exclaimed. "I thought those things only came in cans."

Wednesdays must be blamed for a taste that puts me in a definite minority. I like liver and onions.

Thursday brought on our favorite of all favorites, fried chicken, mashed potatoes and cream gravy. Later on, as times got better, this evolved into chicken-fried steak. My mother took to her grave the know-how for the greatest chicken-fried steak in the history of the universe.

Friday's mainstay is still one I insist on whenever possible, pinto beans and cornbread.

This opened the door for all kinds of embellishments. As a novice, I mixed my beans with mayonnaise. During high school days, I graduated to heavy helpings of my grandmother's chow-chow. This prepared the way for today's mixture with picante sauce.

Leftover cornbread delighted Daddy. His favorite way to celebrate the occasional Friday night victory by the Muleshoe Mules was a post-game helping of crumbled cornbread in a tall glass of "sweet milk."

For years, hamburgers signaled Saturdays. They were homemade or devoured on a stool at Collins Café. Either way, they were the stuff good memories are made of.

Somewhere along the way, the burgers took a back seat to Mexican food. My first taste came in the form of tamales, bought from a handcart pushed down our Main Street on Saturdays by a black entrepreneur from Clovis, New Mexico. Mother learned to make green-chile enchiladas that would make a strong man sweat on top of his head. The ultimate treat was a 30-mile trip to El Monterey in Clovis for a helping of tacos, enchiladas, sopapillas and Mexican hot chocolate. Eventually, half of Muleshoe seems to have joined in that weekly pilgrimage.

As long as our father lived, no one messed with his Sunday menu: pot roast cooked with potatoes, onions and carrots. Cold roast beef sandwiches even made Sunday leftovers special.

With this kind of predictability, our lives stayed on a pretty even keel, not unlike that of the little boy down the block who didn't talk until he was five years old. His folks just assumed that he couldn't talk; then one morning he blurted out, "This oatmeal is lumpy."

"Johnny, you can talk!" exclaimed his stunned mother.

"Certainly," he replied.

"Why have you waited until now?" she asked

"This is the first time anything has gone wrong," he explained.

Petty Theft and Talking Pigs

EARLY ON, I CULTIVATED TECHNIQUES DE-
signed to serve me well if I had chosen to
pursue a life of crime. My childhood philoso-
phy was, "Steal a little bit at a time, and no one will
ever miss it." It never occurred to me that if a little
stuff is stolen long enough, there will be no more stuff.

My pilfering was confined to my mother's kitchen,
and I maintained a strict rule of immediately eating
any evidence. My targets included raisins, brown
sugar, dried apricots and peaches. Brown sugar and
dried apricots were my passions. I was addicted to
them. My cravings for them drew me to the kitchen as
a bear is drawn to honey.

Fear of Mother's wrath, however, assured practiced caution. Stealth and deceit were my tools. The
rule was never to take more than one lump of sugar or
more than one piece of dried fruit at a time. If someone surprised me, the sugar would melt while I en-

gaged the intruder in innocent conversation. The fruit was more of a challenge. Talking, while holding it inconspicuously in my mouth, gave rise to the family assumption that my voice began changing at a very early age.

Alas, my criminal career was cut short by my mother's superior investigative instincts. The beginning of my downfall was her declaration to me, "I just can't believe that I've used so much brown sugar already." What she said with her eyes took all the sweetness out of my pursuit.

Apricots finally got me. Our house detective surprised me the first time I broke my own rule. It was impossible to successfully secrete two pieces in my jaws and carry on a normal conversation. Instead of wrath, I got a warning that gave me food for thought. She said, "You are not supposed to eat those until they've soaked overnight in water. Can you imagine what it is going to do to you if you keep eating those dry?"

Imagination was not something that I had in short supply. Over the next few days, I worked on her challenge. My conclusion closed the door to the fruit cabinet. I envisioned a stomach full of once-dry apricots swelling until I exploded. I had heard about people eating until they popped; now it made sense.

After these thwarted forays and constantly hearing my father say, "Crime doesn't pay," I decided to walk the straight and narrow.

About the time of my reformation, I overheard a conversation in my father's barber shop that made me believe that every now and then the Crime, Inc., payroll department does cut some slack for slow learners. From what I was able to pick up on from a deputy sheriff getting his weekly trim, it went something like this: Farmers on the eastern edge of Bailey County had been missing pigs. No one in the adjacent county had reported any pork poaching. This led the sheriff's sleuths to conclude that the rustlers were invading their territory.

On a moonless autumn night, county and state officers manned roadblocks at every exit from the county. Shortly after midnight, two not-so-bright brothers rumbled down a dirt farm road in an old Plymouth coupe. Between them, on the seat, was a prize porker. In a county sheriff's car, just ahead, waited two of the thieves' sleepy intellectual cousins.

When their headlights picked up the barricade, the hoodlums panicked. "Oh, no, Sam! They've got us dead to rights. What are we going to do?" blubbered the short scruffy guy on the passenger's side.

"Quick, throw your jacket around the pig's shoulders, slap your hat on his head and follow my lead," commanded the husky driver.

Moments later, deputy Leroy shined his flashlight into the squinting eyes of three silent figures. "Hey, buddy, what's your name?"

"Sam Smith," grumbled the driver.

"And you, over there, who are you?"

"B-B-Bob Smith," came back the shaky reply.

"O.K., there in the middle, shorty, what do they call you?"

With perfect timing, Sam drove his right elbow into the ribs of the startled pig. A sharp "Oink!" split the air.

As the taillights of the coupe disappeared in a cloud of dust on the other side of the county line, Leroy turned to his partner and declared, "I've seen some ugly people in my day, but that Oink Smith has got to top the list."

The Mystified Magi

C HRISTMAS IS UNMATCHED FOR TRIGGER-
ing memories. The world reserves no mercy
for the grinch whose eyes do not mist, and
whose heart does not melt when a star blinks from
the top of the water tower, and when Bing Crosby's
rendition of "White Christmas" resonates from a shop
doorway.

For me, the first hearing of a Salvation Army bell
or the first sighting of tinsel on a lamppost releases a
flood of Yuletide reminiscences: Stepping out into the
crisp December air of a West Texas late afternoon, after shopping with my mother for cowboy boots, which
she "might tell Santa about." Long hours browsing
through the thick Sears and Roebuck catalog, after
which no want list could remain modest. Listening as
"Amos 'n' Andy," "Fibber McGee and Molly," Archie at
"Duffy's Tavern," Henry on "The Aldrich Family" and
"The Great Gildersleeve" prepared to celebrate. Press-

ing my nose against a cold back-seat window, while being driven home from a Sunday School Christmas party, and marveling at a very bright star in the winter sky.

There were no artificial trees to be found in our house. The final confirmation that the season had begun was when Daddy arrived for supper with a fragrant evergreen in tow. He would nail crisscrossing boards to the tree's base and work until it stood straight before our parlor's large picture window. The rest of the evening saw the entire family bonded in a labor of love. Certain ornaments survived year after year. Cardboard cutouts from school crafts, before Christmas was banned from the classroom, had special favor with our mother. The crowning moment came when the aging, but never retired, angel was placed on the top branch. Of course, the final task was the search for the one elusive bulb that kept a whole string from blinking. For more than an hour, we would alternate between standing in the street to proudly watch, and sitting in an otherwise dark parlor, being warmed by the dazzle of light, color and reflection. The evening's ceremony was officially over when Mother served the season's first nutmeg-sprinkled cups of eggnog.

A sip of the rich, creamy mixture signaled open season on nibbling, munching, snacking, sneaking and tasting. There was no lack of selections. My maternal grandmother offered an unending supply of date loaf, sweet and sumptuous enough to lock itself forever in your memory. Mother kept a big bowl filled with what she called "chicken feed." It was a salty, garlic-laced mixture of Wheat Chex®, broken pretzels and nuts, all toasted to irresistible perfection. My personal Waterloo was Mother's world-class peanut brittle. It was to be found in a crystal bowl on the coffee table. I found it early and often. My greatest discovery was how well it went with a glass of cold milk.

My pre-Christmas memories are clouded only by the bad experience of rehearsing for an elementary school Christmas program. Daily, our herd of reluctant urchins was marched onto the stage of the high school gymnasium. For an hour, we were drilled in the singing of lyrics that remain my least favorite: "You better watch out; You better not cry; You better not pout; I'm telling you why; Santa Claus is coming to town."

It was while reading the pale-blue mimeographed lines of this ditty, designed to scare kids into abnormal behavior, that I learned once and for all that I am tone deaf and cannot carry a tune. Ever since that experience, any request that I sing anything immediately triggers the memory of a teacher saying, "Now, let's get it right this time." I never did.

Our pitiful pageantry was surpassed only when a Bailey County rural church, desperate for enough people to stage a Christmas program, drafted three awkward cowboys to portray the Three Wise Men. These ranch hands were baffled when their foreman's wife, and church pianist, told them to be sure to dress like the oriental magi. "Ma'am," stammered a lean, raw-boned young man. "How do y'all reckon we gonna know jest how them fellers looked?"

In exasperation, she said, "Read the Bible and figure it out."

A week later, the members of the little church were stunned when the trio stomped up to the hay-filled manger wearing helmets and coats borrowed from the Muleshoe Volunteer Fire Department. Immediately after the program, the irate pianist was in their faces demanding, "What in the world did you think you were doing dressed like that?"

"Well, ma'am," a small, bowlegged man drawled from behind a drooping mustache. "You told us we might git some idy from tha Bible 'bout tha duds them ole boys wore. As ya know, we ain't too good at findin' stuff in tha Good Book, so I asked tha parson. He said that there weren't a whole lot to help us, but that those wise guys come from a far. We figgered that bein' tha case, they musta been far fighters."

Layaways and Fruitcakes

A S BOYS, MY BROTHER, DUDLEY, AND I never had to worry about getting gifts at Christmas. This left a lot more time for us to worry about giving. It didn't take me long to discover that the latter was as much fun as the first, if not more. After Thanksgiving, as the wrapped boxes accumulated under our dazzling tree, our dreams had no limits. Our anticipation of what we might find in the mystery boxes was mingled with that of seeing the response to what we knew was in other boxes.

My first job, shining shoes in Daddy's barber shop, made possible my first big Christmas shopping venture. Late on an October afternoon, I walked the two blocks from the shop to a jewelry store. As I stood in the twilight and stared at the Victorian lamp in the window, I knew little about credit buying. My only experience was when, as a five-year-old, I had bought my girlfriend an ice cream cone at Damron's Drug Store and charged it to my father.

It took all of my courage to approach a formidable-looking saleslady and meekly ask, "How much is that lamp in the window?" I must have looked stunned when I heard her answer, "Thirty-five dollars." For a guy getting 20¢ for shining a pair of boots, that sounded like a fortune. Sensing my despair, she asked, "Would you like to put it on layaway?" Puzzled, I asked, "How does that work?"

On Christmas Eve, I kept the last of six weekly appointments with that helpful lady. This time I departed with a present that still graced my mother's parlor when she died. That lamp's soft rose glow warms me with the memory of the joy of giving.

All of that is not to say that I was opposed to the idea of getting. Early on, I learned "Ask, and you shall receive." It is easy for me to identify with the kid in the popular movie *A Christmas Story*, because I, too, asked for a Red Ryder lever-action Daisy® BB gun. I also was told, "You'll shoot an eye out." I, too, found the trusty weapon among Santa's loot.

Three categories of gifts have left indelible impressions on my passions, personality and preferences. Our first Christmas in our new house, which my parents literally built, was celebrated by the arrival of a cocker spaniel puppy, the first of many dogs in my life.

Books were the second great gift tradition. Mother gave them and, until we were through the third grade, Daddy read them to us. The consistent theme of these volumes cultivated my passion for animals, cowboys and the Great American West. I especially remember *Black Beauty, Lassie Come-Home, My Friend Flicka, Thunderhead, The Green Grass of Wyoming, Riders of the Purple Sage, Wild Fire* and *Smoky, The Cowhorse.*

Will James' *Smoky* and Fred Harman's comic strip, "Red Ryder," nurtured my desire to be a great Western-life artist. James' book was full of his own illustrations, and Harman's depiction of his carrot-headed cowboy hero and his young Apache sidekick, Little Beaver, were in a similar style. The artistic drive took me through high school doing covers for the school paper. Any talent was not polished by training, but I remain a Western-art junkie who itches every time I see a drawing pad or pencil.

Kids often loathe clothes as gifts, but those I received fit my body and my fantasies. Boots dominated, followed by blue jeans, hand-tooled belts and Western-styled shirts. I can remember every pair of boots. Their fancy stitching and the grain of their leather were memorized during long hours of polishing and buffing. When I'm away from home, I can't wait to come home from the airport, shed my suit and tie and slip into the comfort zone of old jeans and well-worn boots.

Mother's annual gift to the whole family has confirmed my conviction that Christmas presents have a shaping influence on our lives. During the summer, she began her annual collection of candied fruit, nuts and a combination of rich ingredients known only to her. Every autumn, those goodies were mixed into a high-calorie concoction, baked into a cake and an aging process started. Periodically, her creation was wrapped in a towel and soaked in a way that was only whispered about in our Baptist home. By Christmas, the fruitcake was ready to take its place in a long line of Christmas delights that are enshrined in my memory's hall of fame.

Each year, the season's first pieces of fruitcake and cups of eggnog were served to celebrate hanging the last ornament on the Christmas tree. From that moment, I awoke each morning anticipating my after-dinner slice. These rich morsels were the last snack of the night well past New Year's Day every year.

Mother's 1980 fruitcake is the last one that I remember. It was special. I took its remaining fragments with me to Uganda, in East Africa. They were shared with a select group of fellow adventurers on a magnificent afternoon, as our launch wallowed in the spray at the foot of Murchison Falls on the Nile River.

My mother's scrumptious creations are only memories, but Christmas isn't complete without a fruitcake. This tradition makes it impossible for me to understand the lack of esteem some people have for them. I feel like someone is kicking my dog when I hear a TV comedian say, "You know that there is really only one fruitcake in the whole world, and it is simply passed from one person to another as an unwanted gift."

I can remember my amazement when a local rancher plopped down in Daddy's barber chair and declared, "I just did the impossible. I got rid of my mother-in-law's fruitcake without having to eat a bite."

"How did you do that?" asked a farmer, who was loafing in my shine chair.

"It weren't easy. My wife warned me that if I threw it out, one of the hands would see it and talk to the wrong person. That had me in a real tizzy until I got this brainstorm before having to go to Lubbock to pick up a new saddle. I just got one of those fancy boxes that the wife and kids were putting presents in. I stuffed that cake in it, tied a ribbon around it and dropped it in the back of my pickup. When I got to Lubbock, I parked in front of Hemphill-Wells department store and spent an hour looking at their Stetson hats. When I came back, somebody had picked up the biggest surprise they'll be getting this Christmas."

Christmas Tradition

F OR ME TO DISCUSS CHRISTMAS TRADITION
Calls for a lot of romantic admission.
I'm guilty on every count.
Bring on the tinsel; I can take any amount.

Strains of "White Christmas" put me in a trance.
Once through "Jingle Bells," and I'm ready to dance.
I declare open season on peanut brittle,
Losing all care that it goes to my middle.

Trim the tree, and do it quite early.
Take it down before the Super Bowl, and I'll get surly.
You frown and say you hate fruitcake?
Give it to me, and you'll my Christmas make.

CHRISTMAS TRADITION

Clean the hearth and decorate the mantle.
Bring in the Yule log and all the wood you can handle.
Put a candle before each pane,
And hope that flakes soon fall on our lane.

With nog and the singing of Bing and Gene,
Before a crackling fire I become serene,
Musing about the ones I used to know,
And imagining sleigh bells in the snow.

Call it commercial and say you've had enough.
Cry out against catalogs, sales and stuff;
But leave me alone if you gripe and rave.
It's an overdose of Christmas tradition I crave.

Going to the Dogs

O F ALL THE ANIMALS IN GOD'S WORLD, only the dog seems especially created with man in mind. Start walking back through history, and wherever you find people, you find dogs. The best guess is that it all started when a wolf was drawn to the smell of cooking meat on a cold night, and some soft-hearted primitive made the mistake of tossing him a bone. The beast probably decided to hang around and make the most of a good thing. Before long, a match was made. Today it may be a schnauzer instead of a lobo, but a lot of folks are still tossing scraps from the table.

Just mention the word "dog" in a public place, and you'll immediately pick up some information about the folks around you. I've always looked at a guy with some suspicion when I hear him say he has no use for dogs.

Whether you take them or leave them, it's hard to talk without mentioning them. Think about it. We say that "every dog has his day." An unsavory villain is called "a dirty dog." Soldiers are called "dog faces." A child is accused of "dogging" his mother's steps. Everyone knows about the "dog days of summer." You may have heard some frazzled soul describe his predicament as "a dog's life." I've heard folks faithful to their political party described as "yellow dog" Democrats or Republicans. In other words, they would just as soon vote for a yellow dog as for a candidate from the opposing party.

Dogs rival people when it comes to acquiring celebrity status. Who hasn't heard of Lassie, Rin Tin Tin, Ole Yeller, Old Shep, Goofy, Precious Pup, Marmaduke, Daisy, Howard Huge and Snoopy? Now, a new cartoon character, Buckles, is making his bid for fame.

When I was a boy, if somebody at our house decided to "go to the dogs," they didn't have far to go. I can't remember a time when one or two of "man's best friends" didn't have a claim to membership in our family. One of my earliest photographs shows me having my shorts tugged by a bug-eyed Boston terrier named Bo.

A parti-colored cocker spaniel came into our lives at a time when a book and its spinoff movie were at the peak of popularity. She joined thousands of other late '40s canines being named Lassie. Her heir was her red, mischievous son, Elmer. He was named after Daisy's pup from "Blondie" cartoon fame.

My high school days were marked by the reign of a hyperactive toy Manchester terrier, Chico. She arrived as a Christmas present and assured herself a lasting place in the memories or our extended family by mistaking the trousers, which a visiting uncle had neatly folded and left on the floor beside his bed, for the newspapers on which she was being housebroken. She was still around when I brought my future wife, Robbie, home from college. The jealous mutt again made sure that she would not be forgotten by sitting between this strange young woman and me, and growling when we held hands. An unbroken line of family dogs has continued to Nikki, the Siberian husky that lies at my feet now as I write and read.

Tell me who you are and what you do, and I can find a dog that was bred with you in mind. There are cow dogs, sheep dogs, ride-in-the-back-of-a-pickup dogs, attack dogs, companion dogs, seeing-eye dogs, bomb- or drug-sniffing dogs, show dogs, coon dogs, bird dogs, sled dogs and lap dogs.

By stroking a dog, you can lower your blood pressure. A good dog can take the place of a psychiatrist. It's a lot cheaper, and you can tell it anything without fearing that it will think less of you.

With many a "good ole boy," his dogs rank just behind his truck and just ahead of his wife and children. I heard about a fellow who got agitated because his sons were wandering too far from the confines of their yard. He threw open a screen door and yelled, "You kids git outta that road! You're gonna git ever' dog I got run over."

No real dog man is above exaggerating about his animal's intelligence or ability. This is especially true of men who hunt with a four-footed companion at their sides. One West Texas farmer just filled time from one quail season to another. His pride and joy was a pointer who was dependable as sunrise. It's impossible to imagine his surprise and embarrassment when a feed store bull session erupted into laughter. To his utter consternation, the dog at his side was frozen in a point on one of the men in the group huddled around a Coke® machine.

"Huh, that hound of yours don't know a quail from a cowboy," teased the store's owner.

"I'll have to admit that this here is flabbergastin'," said the dog's baffled master. Rubbing his chin whiskers, he turned to the object of the point. "Say, Mister, what's your name?"

Smiling, the man said, "Bob White."

I reckon that owner's relief could be matched only by the surprise of the guy who took his new retriever duck hunting. When the yellow Lab leapt from the boat to fetch his first downed mallard, he trotted easily across the top of the water and returned without even getting his tail wet.

Amazed, the hunter turned to a cynical companion and asked, "Wow, what do you think of that?"

Shrugging, he said, "The poor sucker can't swim a lick, can he?"

Gone Fishing

WHEN I THINK BACK TO GROWING UP IN Muleshoe, on the South Plains of West Texas, I have absolutely no regrets. Having said that, I've got to admit that there were some built-in limitations. Certain things just weren't easy to learn, like how to fish. To find much water out there, you've got to dig a pretty deep hole. I reckon there might be three-year-old fish in Bailey County that don't know how to swim.

My mother had a zest for going against the grain and messing with the ordinary. To say that she liked to fish would miss the truth as much as saying that a bee kinda likes honey. She had an absolute passion for fishing, and if the crappie and catfish wouldn't come to where she was, she would go to them. She was in the vanguard of the folks who ventured out of Muleshoe to test the shores and depths of Possum Kingdom and Buffalo Shoals.

She never lost her enthusiasm for angling. After my father died, she talked a lady friend into climbing aboard a single-engine airplane with her. They were flown to a lake in the interior of Mexico. Every day for a week, they joined a group of Alabama car salesmen in catching enough bass to feed an army. Her last day on earth was spent with a rod and reel in her hands, doing what she liked best.

For some reason, I just never caught the fishing fever. I did, however, hear enough stories to equip me to trade yarns with the best of those folks who spend their lives pursuing the big one. Most of what I learned about the sport came from hanging out in Daddy's barber shop. Of course, that meant that fish, fact and fiction got real mixed up in my understanding. Sorting it all out never seemed very important to the sources of my knowledge, so I never gave it much thought.

Most of the fish stories I heard were about the ones that got away. Maybe that's why I'll never forget hearing about the one that didn't. In the words of the storyteller, it went something like this:

"When we bought our farm, the pond in the south pasture hadn't been fished for several years. We didn't disturb anything either until my baby brother came home from the war and decided to heal his mind at the holding end of a cane pole.

"One night he rushed in late for supper and breathlessly announced that he had just tied into the biggest fish of his life. 'Did ya land 'im?' asked Dad.

"'No way,' he said. 'He took my hooks and sinkers three times. I'll try again tomorrow. Man, he's big, really big!'

"Within a week, the word was out all over the county. At first it was just weekends, then it was every day. Folks came from everywhere. They arrived determined and left defeated. That old fish wasn't just big; he could fight. Everybody lost their hooks and sinkers. After a while, the little store where you turned off the highway to come to our house couldn't keep hooks and sinkers.

"It was a blazing hot July afternoon when I had to report to Dad, 'We've got a dead pig out there. What d'ya want ta do with it?'

"My brother looked up from adjusting a tractor seat. With a gleam in his eyes he said, 'Let me have it.'

"'What fer?', asked Dad

"'You'll see,' he said. 'This may be just what I've been lookin' for.'

"We watched in quiet amazement as he first tied a cable to a large grappling hook and attached the other end to the plow hitch on the tractor. Next, the tractor was driven to the bank of the pond and the deceased pig was threaded as bait onto the hook. With a heave, the pork was tossed into the water.

"Almost immediately, the pond churned with activity. Before the tractor could be started, it was slipping toward the water. Just in time, my brother got it going and slowly pulled his prize to the surface and finally onto dry ground.

"It was the biggest fish anyone had ever seen, but we couldn't eat it. It was so full of hooks and sinkers that we had to sell it for scrap iron."

Hearing that story made me start believing that catching the big one may not necessarily open the door to satisfaction. Two other yarns settled it. After hearing them, I knew you could get what you wanted and either end up with more than you could handle or less than you had seen.

The first one was about two good ole boys from Bailey County who drove eight hours to get to one of those good lakes below the Caprock, and then they fought this big fish for half the night. Tuckered out, one of them reckoned as to how they might stop trying to pull him in and just back up to him. It worked, but when their flashlights picked out an eye on each side of the boat, they just cut the line and quietly slipped away.

My favorite story is from one of Mother's bass-fishing adventures. While casting in a quiet inlet, she noticed a willow branch gently dipping toward the water in a soft breeze. The flickering leaves were casting their shadows on the surface.

To Mother's amazement, every time the branch dipped down, a huge trophy bass leaped up. "Why, he thinks those are June bug shadows," she laughed. Timing her cast between leaps, she landed her prize. As she netted the fish, she said, "You're going to make me famous!"

Before long, however, her celebration turned to bewilderment. Her trophy weighed every bit of six ounces. It all made sense when she cleaned the sucker. It was plumb chock-full of June bug shadows.

Just for the Fun of It

JUST ABOUT EVERYBODY HAS HEARD ABOUT the frustrated hedonist who complained, "Everything I like to do is illegal, immoral or fattening."

While most of us have little sympathy with the first two aspects of his gripe, we might side with him on the latter. Today, I eat to control my weight and my cholesterol, to regulate my intake of fiber and sodium, and to be sure I'm getting enough iron and calcium, I really can't remember the last time I ate guilt-free just for the fun of it.

God built fun into what it takes to get us here and what it takes to keep us here. However, from the moment we get here, somebody is warning us that if we don't straighten up and watch what we eat, we're not going to get to stay long. This reminds me of the story I heard about the elderly gentleman who died and went to heaven. He was met by his wife who had preceded him in death. "Oh, Honey, isn't this wonderful?" she asked.

"Yes, it is," he replied. "And if it hadn't been for all those oat bran muffins you stuffed us with, we would've been here a lot sooner."

If you don't think eating should be fun, ask anyone about the things they enjoy doing the most. Any honest person will include eating something on the list.

Now, don't get sick or report me to the "Correct Eating Police," but here are some things from childhood which I remember eating and drinking just for the fun of it.

At my grandmother's table, I remember spooning sugar from the bottom of my iced-tea glass, crunching the fried batter off a pully bone, taking a big piece of angel food cake and eating the icing first, mixing sorghum molasses and real butter, and taking the last piece of bacon from a breakfast platter.

From our family fixings, I remember chicken-fried steak and cream gravy, deep-fried catfish and hush puppies, over-easy eggs with red-eye gravy and cathead biscuits, lemon pie, made from Eagle Brand® milk with graham cracker crust, and sweet potato casserole with lots of marshmallows. Of course, the real fun stuff had absolutely no redeeming virtues. Some of it, even a 1940s or '50s mother knew to warn you away from.

Sometimes the goodness of these things was enhanced because they were on a forbidden list, especially at school. What 55-and-better man can't remember seeing just how long he could get away with stashing a giant jawbreaker in his mouth during science class? That was always an interesting experiment.

Then there were the bizarre snacks that could be carried into a schoolroom in your pocket. Orange Kool-Aid® could be surreptitiously licked from your hand when the teacher was facing the blackboard. The problem was that before long, both your palm and tongue said, "This kid has been up to no good."

Among the best things ever invented for sneaking into school were those little paraffin bottles full of sweet red or green liquid. The guy who invented those might have envisioned kids' popping these into their little mouths intact and munching the liquid and wax together.

Only the most totally uncool nerd would have ever done that. Proper procedure called for biting the top from the bottle, catching the teacher not looking, toasting a buddy across the room, downing the drink, then chewing the bottle. The next time the teacher turned around, a really thoughtful guy would toss a bottle across the room so that his friend could return the toast.

Anybody with a little imagination could get away with chewing Doublemint® during study hall. It took the really daring to survive peeling a plug of Fleer's

Dubble Bubble®, not coughing on the first rush of sweetness, and blowing a big one while passing the comic strip wrapper to the guy across the aisle.

Other "sneak 'em when you could" school treats included licorice ropes (if you were looking for a real mess), candy corn (I always bit the yellow tip off first) and Tootsie® Rolls. The Tootsie® Roll challenge was to resist chewing and make one last for a whole class period. Two playground favorites were candy cigarettes and bubble gum cigars, pretty good indicators that the tobacco folks were targeting kids a long time before anybody thought up "Joe Camel."

A lot of the fun food that I remember offered all kinds of ways to develop and express individuality. There's no telling how soon a child locks in on his or her own method of dealing with an Oreo® cookie. My m.o. has always been to open the little buggers, carefully lick away the white filling and then dunk the chocolate sections in a glass of milk.

These idiosyncrasies carried over into a whole array of weird fun food habits. I ate a nickel box of peanuts one nut at a time, carefully sucking the peeling off of each nut first. I could make a Baby Ruth® last forever by first licking away the chocolate, then eating the peanuts and finally munching the candy heart bit by bit.

Of course, I participated in the common practices of pouring salted peanuts into my Coke®, always drinking RC Cola® while eating a Moon® Pie, and never giving up hope that the prize in my next box of Cracker Jack® would be better than the last ten zillion. I never tired of traveling across America with a bunch of friends by comparing the towns on the bottoms of Coke® bottles. I loved to join my grandmother in having a Dr. Pepper® at ten, two and four.

When I start thinking like this, a bunch of stuff starts yelling for my attention: m&m's®, picture-show popcorn, Big Red® soda pops, Fig Newtons®, Hershey's® bars, red hots and chocolate-covered cherries. The first time I got enough money to splurge on a whole box of those little jaw lockers, I found out that yes, you can get too much of a good thing.

Isn't it interesting that our national obsession with stress seems to coincide with legislated proper nutrition. Most of the folks I talk to complain that they're suffering from stress, and these same people vow that they're eating by the book. I believe that your diet will either create or combat stress. If you've gotten to the place where you just can't cope, let me suggest a proven anti-stress diet. The dietician is unknown.

For breakfast, you can have one-half grapefruit, one slice of whole wheat toast and eight ounces of skim milk. At lunch, eat four ounces of lean broiled chicken breast with one cup of steamed zucchini. Finish by nibbling one Oreo® cookie and sipping a cup of herb tea. Enjoy a mid-afternoon snack by eating the rest of the Oreo® cookies, from the package, with a quart of Rocky Road ice cream, eaten from the carton and topped with a jar of hot fudge. At dinner, finish a perfect day with two loaves of garlic bread, one large mushroom-and-pepperoni pizza, two liters of root beer, three Snickers® bars and one frozen cheesecake, eaten directly from the freezer.

Bon appetit—and chill out!

Muleshoe's Song

I T'S STRANGE HOW AN OPPOSITE MOMENT AND circumstance can frame a memory of time and place. On a crisp, still autumn morning, while watching the Ohio River flow by Huntington, West Virginia, I recalled songs that this water and the surrounding hills had inspired. In my heart, another song replaced the calm with wind and the mountains with plains and sky.

West Texas wind 'round a window sill
Singing a song; I can hear it still,
High above the Brazos breaks
Where far horizons no limits take.

Stinging cold and blistering heat
Hurled challenges only the strong did meet.
Bold pioneers on a rolling sea of grass,
Islands of farms and ranches prove their will to last.

MULESHOE'S SONG

Flood and drought cruelly took their turn.
Crops, buildings and dreams would suddenly burn.
Fiery bolts, twisting wind and killing hail
Drove the weak to lose their hope and fail.

Men and women who dared to stay
Conquered land and elements to earn dismay.
In reward, Earth gave up water from its depth;
Windmills harnessed power from the Plains' strong
        breath.

Hereford cattle came and grazed
Where bison herds had men amazed.
Railroad tracks and loading chutes
Were seeds from which towns took roots.

Plains that had heard the Comanche cry
Saw grain elevators reach for the sky.
Prairies where buffalo wolves did prowl
Gave up grain and cotton in response to plow.

Merchants, barbers, doctors and preachers came.
Teachers, saddle makers and printers did the same.
Shops, churches and schools stood in sharp contrast
Where massive sky and vast expanse reached to meet
        at last.

From this field of grass and sands
My hometown grew, and today it stands.
Built by the best that strong men and women do,
It's the pride of the Plains; it's Muleshoe.

West Texas wind 'round a window sill,
Singing a song; I can hear it still,
A song of faith and will for the strong and few,
Who still build and grow in Muleshoe.

West Texas wind 'round a window sill,
Singing a song; I can hear it still.
Reaching out, Muleshoe's song
Calls me back where I belong.

Muleshoe, World Famous

SINCE GRADUATING FROM MULESHOE HIGH School in 1955, I've traveled clear across the U.S.A. and around the world. I've met thousands of people from every walk of life. I've seldom been anywhere that someone has not heard of my hometown.

A barber in Syracuse, New York, asked, "Where are you from?" When I said that I was from Muleshoe, Texas, he looked astonished and said, "Hey, I was in the army with a guy from there."

On a beautiful February day, I sat down to lunch with new friends in Kisumu, Kenya, on the shore of Lake Victoria. I dined on fried chicken, mashed potatoes, cream gravy, homemade rolls and sliced tomatoes. While eating, we talked about Muleshoe. Of the six people at the table, everyone had grown up within 30 miles of the county seat of Bailey County.

From Rio to Rome and from Portland to Pensacola, folks know about my hometown. A postcard has been on sale there for many years. It pictures a preppie little boy in shorts, knee-high socks, blazer and beanie, holding a balloon. He's being confronted by another kid, decked out in jeans, boots and a cowboy hat, who is asking, "Do y'all mean to stand there and tell me you never heard of Muleshoe, Texas?"

Most people have. I was reminded of this when I met Jim Craig in Stuttgart, Arkansas. Jim's in the business of selling seeds to farmers. When he heard me mention Muleshoe, his eyes lit up and he asked, "Did you ever know a man named Rufus Gilbreth?"

"Sure," I said. "He did the same thing in Muleshoe that you do here."

From there, Jim launched into a yarn that may be fact or fiction, but to me it wasn't surprising. It seems that Rufus was in New York City for a convention and was staying at the famous Waldorf Astoria Hotel. On his arrival, he went to the newsstand off the lobby and handed six copies of the *Muleshoe Journal* to the startled man behind the counter.

Rufus said, "Hang onto these. In a little while, I'm going to come in here and ask for a copy. I'll hand you $5 and, if you'll play it straight and act like we've never seen each other, you can keep the change."

An hour later, he strolled across the lobby on his way to dinner with five other seed dealers from around the country. Stopping in front of the newsstand, he said, "Hang on a minute, boys. I'm gonna step in here and see if I can get a copy of this week's Muleshoe paper."

Hooting, whistling, laughing and slapping each other on the back, the conventioneers followed Rufus up to the counter. When he asked for the *Muleshoe Journal*, they poked each other and rolled their eyes. Without cracking a smile, the shopkeeper said, "I got one left. It's hard as all get out to keep these things."

Tucking his paper under his arm, Rufus handed over a five dollar bill and said, "Keep the change."

As he left the hotel, his buddies were still standing in the lobby scratching their heads.

My nomination for the best "Muleshoe and the World" story dates back to one that I first heard as a boy in Daddy's barber shop. There was a guy, that we will call Joe McDoogal, who was a frequent shoeshine and shave customer. Daily he bombarded everybody within hearing distance with his bragging about where he had been and the people he knew. If anyone mentioned a place or person, no matter how remote or famous, Joe's response was, "Been there and know him."

He finally crossed the line on a busy Saturday afternoon. The shop was packed, and the conversations touched on just about every subject known to man. Somebody made a passing comment about the Pope. Joe stopped everyone in mid-sentence by saying, "Ah, yes, the Pope. I know him well."

"That's it, Joe," said a cynical rancher. "I'm ready to bet $100 that you don't know the Pope."

Before you could blink an eye, there was a groundswell of response. Just about everybody in the shop wanted to get in on the action, and the bet grew to a jackpot amount. Undaunted, Joe stood his ground. Finally, someone asked the inevitable question, "How're we ever gonna prove this one way or the other?"

"Take all this money you're talking about and send me to Rome," said Joe. "If I can't get an audience with the Pope and prove that I know him, I'll pay you back."

"That would still be taking your word for it," somebody protested.

A local banker, who had been observing the whole thing, said, "I'll tell you what; I'll go with him and make sure we get the straight of it."

Sure enough, within a week Joe and the banker had driven to Amarillo and flown to Dallas, New York and Rome. Everybody in Muleshoe was figuring that it was going to be well worth the expense to shut Joe up once and forever.

At the Vatican, things hit a snag when the West Texas pilgrims learned that they could secure a papal audience for only one person. Obviously, that person would have to be Joe. His banker chaperone figured he was back to square one. "How in the world am I gonna know if the Pope really knows you?" he asked Joe.

Rev. Samuel J. King's family (c 1920) from the left: Spurgeon, Josie, Ethel, Sam and Mabel (Wayne's mother).

"Sister Josie" and "Uncle Sam" (Wayne's maternal grandparents).

Mabel and Clinton Bristow, Wayne's parents (c 1937), soon after moving to Muleshoe.

Brother King, ready to go preach again.

Mabel and Clinton Bristow (c 1935).

Wayne in the arms
of his "Auntie" Ethel.

Wayne and his first dog, Bo (c 1938).

Baby Wayne (c 1936).

Wayne and his brother, Dudley.

Wayne in the first grade.

Wayne as a freshman at Muleshoe
High School.

Wayne with his high school friend,
Tommy Osborn. Tommy had the '41
Ford coupe with the great radio that
is mentioned in "All Night Jazz and
the Baptist Hymnal."

Wayne as an end on the Muleshoe
Mules football team.

Wayne's senior year at Muleshoe
High School, 1955.

Wayne and his father, Clinton Bristow, in front of the barber shop on Muleshoe's Main Street (1955). Wayne's first job was shining shoes in that shop, and the stories he heard from farmers, cowboys and town folks inspired many of the stories in this book. His father gave Wayne and many of his friends their first haircuts and was still there to give many of their children their first trim.

"I'll tell you what I'll do," said Joe. "I'll get him to come out on the balcony with me and wave to you."

Knowing that he had to play the hand he'd been dealt, the banker agreed. Later that day, however, he was amazed to see the size of the crowd that had gathered in the plaza facing the papal apartments. After a long wait, two men came out onto a balcony. Joe's companion immediately recognized him, but he had no idea if the robed man beside Joe was really the person they had traveled halfway around the world to meet. Frustrated, he turned to a small Italian boy, pointed to the waving pair and asked, "Son, is that the Pope up there?"

Squinting his eyes, the boy said, "I don't know if that priest is the Pope, but the man with him is Joe McDoogal from Muleshoe, Texas."

Cuffed Jeans, Turned-up Collars and Poodle Skirts

A GOOD FRIEND HAS A TALENTED DAUGH-ter who put in several seasons singing and dancing at a popular theme park. I was invited to see one of her shows and meet the cast. It was weird. As Yogi Berra said, "It was déja vu all over again."

Here were these '90s young people with duck tails, leather jackets, bobby socks and fuzzy sweaters. Trying to take it all in, I asked myself, "Was it really like this?" Yes, it was, but even more so. You would have had to be there to get it right. These kids were imitating "Happy Days," and "Happy Days" imitated the '50s. This troupe of bebopping performers were twice removed from reality. Sure, the jeans, jackets and sweaters stirred the right memories, but the real stuff is just hard to come by after 40 years. Our '50s high school garb fell into two categories. The first, I would

148

label "Good Memories;" and the second, "Good Riddance."

Let's dredge up the last first, and put it behind us. In this memory file I find pedal pushers (designed to make even Marilyn Monroe look tacky); multiple petticoats (when your date got into the car, you had to beat down a mountain of nylon net for five minutes to find the gear shift); iridescent socks (I had never heard of chartreuse until they came along); new blue jeans with metal buttons (when they had been starched and you were late getting dressed for school, your screams of frustration made your dog hide under the bed); stinky tennis shoes (the odor had to be built in, because everybody's smelled the same); and galoshes with snap-over fasteners (no kid with any sense would be seen dead in a pair).

Now, for the really cool stuff. Once you got the jeans buttoned and broken in, they were the foundation of every neat wardrobe. These weren't the holes-in-the-knee, ragged-bottomed, faded castoffs of the '80s. The blue was dark to contrast with the carefully turned-up cuffs. Everybody's jeans were ironed, and some were creased. A lot of "with it" girls exerted much effort to stitch a crease onto the front legs of their denims. These had a special name known only to teenagers.

Of course, it took the right footwear to complete a teenage fashion statement. Four staples were required: penny loafers (with real pennies inserted), saddle oxfords, white bucks and blue suedes. Each selection was designed to complete a particular look. For instance, the white bucks were perfect with jeans, a white tee shirt and a leather-sleeved letter jacket. Girls used the saddle oxfords to match up with bobby socks, swishing poodle skirts and those soft, short-sleeved fuzzy sweaters. My blue suedes were saved for a special dress-up outfit which included a soft tweed topcoat, which I liked to wear with a turned-up collar and a white silk scarf.

Popular entertainers of the '50s had a strong influence on teenage fashions. Billy Eckstine's high, rolled collars inspired "Mr. B" shirts. They were my favorites.

While the tucked-in duck tail effect at the back of many early rock 'n' roll stars' hair styles got all the press, it was the front that took most of my getting-ready time every morning. Once the hair was oiled, the sides combed back and the tails folded in just right, there remained that all-important curl that had to fall down over the forehead. By fourth period, you had to fight for mirror space in the boys room to keep the look both casual and cool.

My father, being a barber, warred mightily against this decadent hair styling. His specialty was the flattop. It always amazed me that the two groups of guys who seemed to prefer this pre-Marine Corps look were at opposite extremes, football linemen and science class wizards.

Daddy's flattops were good. He even used a ruler to be sure the top was smoothed to an even surface. Unless you got your hair from a porcupine, you had to use a mixture made from axle grease and tar, called Butch Wax, to keep the half-inch of remaining growth upright.

If I had to color the '50s, I would use pink against charcoal gray or black. Music fixed pink and white in the history of the era: "A White Sport Coat and a Pink Carnation" and "Cherry Pink and Apple Blossom White."

Today's mania for billboard tee shirts was unknown in the '50s. White was in, and Marlon Brando made it cool to roll up the sleeves. His movie, *The Wild One*, made every guy I knew want a black leather motorcycle jacket to wear over that plain tee.

Believe it or not, when I was in high school, Lubbock, Amarillo and Clovis didn't have malls. There were no teenage specialty stores. So, where, pray tell, did a cool clotheshorse go to get fitted out? Well, if you had wheels and money, you could go to The Hub in Amarillo or Hemphill-Wells in Lubbock, but St. Clair's or Cobbs in Muleshoe would do just fine. One hometown store could meet every clothing need from the cradle to the grave. How you put it together determined if you were neat or nerd.

Speaking of clothes for the grave, one day while I was flipping through a stack of jeans, I couldn't help overhearing a conversation between a St. Clair's salesclerk and a dejected customer. The poor guy had just been to see Dr. L. T. Green to complain of severe headaches, shortness of breath, bulging eyes, ringing ears and hoarseness. After listening to these woeful symptoms, the good doctor had told his patient to prepare for the worst. So off he went to buy his funeral clothes.

After selecting the best suit and tie, he decided to top everything off with a new white dress shirt. "What size?" asked the clerk.

"I wear a 14-inch collar," he said.

"Oh, no," the clerk protested. "Why, if you tried to wear a 14-inch collar, you'd have bad headaches, your eyes would bulge, your ears would ring, you'd be short of breath and hoarse as all get out."

Wheels

WHEN I WAS A FRESHMAN IN HIGH school, it had been just 43 years since Henry Ford put his first Model-T on the market, but America's love affair with the automobile was already well established. Now it's impossible for me to separate cars from my teenage memories. It wasn't that cars were an absolute necessity for our family in a town where we could walk to anywhere in less than 15 minutes. Our first set of wheels was on a classic 1950 Ford. After that, an auto figured into almost every significant event.

Of course I remember cars before the '50s; I just didn't take them personally. There were my grandfather's Pontiac coupes, which he liked to refer to as "a pony and a hack." There was Mrs. Parker's big black Packard, which she drove as the treasurer of the Church of the Nazarene in Hamlin, Texas, until she was well into her 90s. It probably contained enough metal to build ten cars today. There was the Cadillac which took Tot Laux and my mother on their shopping forays to Clovis, Amarillo and Lubbock, and there were Guy Nickels' pickups which provided rides to many Clovis Pioneers baseball games at Bell Park.

Now that I look back, I have to ask myself if the human race in North America would have slowly ceased to exist after the beginning of the 20th century had it not been for the advent of the automobile. How in the world would anyone have dated, courted and gotten married without a car? I first recognized this necessary bond between cars and girls on the rainy night of my eighth grade graduation. My good friend, Jack Jones, had a generous sister, "Little One," who bravely loaned him her shiny black Oldsmobile for the evening. That night I was introduced to double dating and began a whole new era of my life. After that, I spent a lot less time hanging out with the boys.

This is not to say that cars didn't play a major role in strictly boy things. Their radios provided vital information to any guy shrewd enough to get out of class and make his way to the parking lot during the World Series. They ferried hooky players, bent on wasting their youth, 18 miles to the pool hall on the Texas/New Mexico state line. They fed foolish teen competitiveness late at night on lonely country roads, at the expense of many a father's tires and transmission. Did you know that a 1953 Buick could top 140 miles per hour between section lines?

There were real cars, such as Tommy Osborn's old coupe with a truck radio that could pull in stations from Los Angeles to New Orleans. Then there were the cars of fiction. These were designed to feed my already overactive imagination. The brothers in the Hardy Boys detective books had a roadster. I was never sure just what that was, but it sounded like the perfect vehicle for mystery and heroic escapades.

Jack Benny's Maxwell also baffled me. I had never heard of one until the first time I heard it come up in a conversation between him and Rochester on "The Jack Benny Program." That car was as foreign to my comprehension as a Kaiser would be to a teenager today. It didn't take me long to figure out that Maxwells and dinosaurs had gone the same way.

For beauty and uniqueness, no cars in the world could match those of Batman and the Green Hornet. While the Batmobile has endured to capture the imagination of modern kids, the whirring buzz of the Green Hornet's car is permanently locked in my memory. When bad guys heard that, they knew the jig was up.

Henry Ford initiated a new passage of life. Once the automobile made its debut, getting the keys to the family car became every boy's primary obsession. To accomplish this was to have one foot into manhood. It meant freedom, status and the hope of winning the affection of that one special girl. To be denied the car was so terrible that no teenage boy could even think about it without convulsing in agony.

About the time I finished college, this worst of all calamities fell on a neighbor's son. The '50s were over and the "change-everything" decade of the '60s was dawning. This boy was among the first to fall under its revolutionary influence. This meant that he was one of the first Muleshoe High School students to let his hair length reach below his collar. His irate father declared that there would be no more car keys until there had been a haircut.

"But, Daddy," the boy protested. "If you look at all the pictures people have painted of Jesus, you will see that He had long hair."

"Yes," replied his father. "And if you will read the Bible, you will discover that He walked everywhere He went."

Coping on the Llano Estacado

WHEN PIONEER EXPLORERS STRUGGLED up from the breaks carved out by the twin forks of the Brazos River to the top of the Caprock, running across the bottom of the Texas Panhandle, they were overwhelmed by a seemingly limitless stretch of flat grassland. The landscape was completely without trees, and the only visible water stood in the many buffalo wallows that pocked the prairie. Grass grew higher than the stirrups of saddles, and the first hint of the area's greatest resource was seen as water from a vast aquifer seeped into the ruts left by heavily loaded supply wagons. In the years ahead, this harsh but fruitful country would attract farmers, ranchers and town builders of unusual courage, ingenuity and persistence. One of the first white men ever to see what is now the Texas Panhandle and South Plains was the Spanish explorer Francisco

Coronado. He called it the Llano Estacado, the Staked
Plains.

A sea of golden grass waving in a merciless wind,
An azure globe touching horizons without an end,
Blazing sun and bitter cold, hail from an electric sky,
And crashing thunder that just won't die.

Bison herds taking days to pass
Were at home in a place so vast.
Spanish explorers and their leader Coronado
Called it the Llano Estacado.

With no encouraging mountain on their scope,
These conquistadors soon lost all hope.
A city of gold they could not find
In a wild, flat hazard to body and mind.

The land gave up nothing, but its invaders dearly paid.
When they fled, their mustang ponies in wild herds stayed.
These horses made Comanche warriors free to roam,
And with fierce terror to rule their high plains home.

But their proud time would end.
By sheer force a new era would begin.
First rangers, then troops fought and slew
For what white men said destiny had made their due.

Soon the mustang was mounted by men in saddles.
They first rode for Goodnight, to work his cattle,
Driving longhorns from the Panhandle to Abilene,
And facing storms and critters just plain mean.

Their ranges were the JA, the Matador and the XIT.
They were the last plainsmen to be really free;
But finally wire and brands drew their boundary lines,
And farms and towns were just a matter of time.

Unfettered men shook their heads and turned to the west.
Plows broke up the land, and deep wells gave up their best.
White fields of cotton and a waving sea of grain
Became the scene and work for a new man and his domain.

Dust bowl years humbled men and taught them well.
Again the land had won respect; wise use did it compel.
With grass restored, cattle and crops shared the plains.
Farmers and cowboys found reward in partnership of
    tractor and reins.

Now corporations threaten homesteads and self-reli-
    ance disdain.
Cities call the young from town and country to come
    and remain.
But the plains are still a place of growth and hope
For determined people who have learned to work and cope.

If you will be still and look, you can see even yet,
In the lingering gold of a West Texas sunset,
A glimpse of Cibola in the land of Coronado,
This place he called the Llano Estacado.

As a boy, growing up in Muleshoe and hanging out in my daddy's barber shop, I reckon I heard just about every smart-aleck remark anybody passing through the country could make about our area's topography and climate. If I heard one, I heard a thousand references to the claim that we had nothing between us and the North Pole but a barbed wire fence. We were supposed to have three-year-old fish in Bailey County that didn't know how to swim. Somebody was always bringing up the story about the guy who fainted at a funeral, and the people had to pour sand on his face to bring him around. We were famous for having miles and miles of miles and miles. Now I have to admit, our surroundings didn't do much to discourage this kind of snide consideration. Even the names of towns contributed to the reputation. What comes to mind when you hear about Plainview, Levelland, Earth and Needmore?

Sometimes it was pretty hard to sort out fact and fiction. Personally, I always believed the story about the traveling salesman who pulled into a filling station in Causey, New Mexico, during a howling sandstorm. Tumbleweeds were bouncing off pickup fenders, and the flag at the post office was popping like firecrackers on the Fourth of July. A barefooted, freckle-faced boy, wearing overalls without a shirt, came squinting through the dust to wait on the stranger. Holding on to his hat while he watched the kid fill his gas tank, the salesman asked, "Son, does it ever rain around here?"

Thinking hard, the boy scratched his head and said, "Yes, sir. It rained a quarter of an inch over at Portales year before last, but we didn't get to go that day."

Early on, anybody who has carved out a home and living on the Llano Estacado has learned that coping is the key to survival. Bend, but don't break. Find out what works and make it work for you. Some years ago, I ate lunch with a cowboy on a Panhandle spread who had learned well how to cope. After eating, we were enjoying coffee out on his porch. I was amazed to observe a prairie dog all perked up and staring back at me from inside a chicken wire cage. "Is that a pet?" I asked.

"Kinda," my host replied. "I reckon he's more of a partner."

"How's that?" I asked.

"Well, sir," he said. "That little varmint is the best work saver I ever found. You see, I carry him with me in a saddlebag, and when I need him, I got this little collar and leash, and I use him to dig post holes."

Leaning back and grinning, he said, "The boss ain't figured out yet how I can set posts faster'n he can string wire."

Cross Your Fingers,
Just in Case

H OW MANY TIMES HAVE YOU HEARD someone say, "I'm not superstitious, but...?"

If you're honest, you'll probably have to admit that there are some things you grew up doing and not doing because they held either a threat or a promise. I certainly had my share of these hangups. I absorbed them from a very superstitious housekeeper, a father who was a walking catalog of folklore and an uncle who was such a good kidder that you ended up believing most of what he said.

On a stroll down the Main Street sidewalks of Muleshoe, I must have given the appearance of skipping because I would never dare to step on a crack. I wouldn't hesitate to step out into Saturday afternoon traffic just to avoid walking under a ladder that was propped against a building. I grew up hoping that a year would finally roll around when all the Friday the 13ths would fall on Wednesdays.

On our school playground, at least half the boys had a rabbit's foot stuffed into a pocket of their jeans. None of us would have dared to undertake a dangerous stunt, such as going down the high slide on wax paper, without first knocking on wood. When a buddy said, "Honest injun," you wanted to be standing so that you could see if his fingers were crossed. Only when he crossed his heart and hoped to die could you be absolutely sure he was shooting straight.

Schoolhouses, churches and banks were just about the only buildings in town where a horseshoe couldn't be found over at least one door. Woe unto the person who ever tried to evict a cricket or who attempted to open an umbrella indoors. Your string had run out and you were done for sure if your path was ever crossed by a black cat, or if you broke a mirror. This latter offense guaranteed at least seven years of bad luck. Of course, there might be some hope if you could throw salt over your left shoulder and wish upon a star. At least two rules were firmly observed at our house. You never walked around with one shoe on and one shoe off, and you never failed to eat black-eyed peas on New Year's Day.

Now, I know there are lots of folks who vow that they never bought into any of this superstition business, but sure as daylight, their day of reckoning is coming. Like the two women who came out of St. Clair's dry goods store in Muleshoe on a hot 1950 afternoon and encountered a talking frog. "Kiss me," the frog croaked, "and I'll turn into a dryland cotton farmer."

Before you could blink an eye, one of the women had stuffed the frog into her purse. "Aren't you going to kiss him?" her friend asked.

"Shoot, no!" came the reply. "A talking frog's worth a whole lot more'n a dryland cotton farmer."

A Mountain of Diamonds

AFTER WORLD WAR I FAILED TO MAKE THE world safe for democracy, folks in West Texas started asking about their sons, "How're you gonna keep 'em down on the farm after they've seen Paree?" Until then, only the brave adventurer or the compelled missionary ventured outside the comfort zones of culture and language. The world wars changed that forever. Since the end of the second global conflict, folks have ventured farther and farther from the homestead. Now, we travel from country to country as easily as our grandparents went from county to county.

Most kids who grew up during the '40s and '50s had a father or uncle who could talk from experience about North Africa, Italy, England, France, Germany, the South Seas and the Philippines. One of my most amazing memories is the black-and-white Kodak snapshot of an uncle standing under a palm tree with a sailor's cap cocked to just above his right eyebrow. He was in a place I could only vaguely imagine.

Everybody knows about somebody who will be forever too young, for whom memory and time stopped in one of those far-off places. Thankfully, we also remember those who braved the hell of war and came home to town, farm or ranch. The most exhilarating moment I've ever witnessed was when my next-door friend's father came walking up the street with a duffle bag over his shoulder, home from the war.

Being home was good enough for most of these veterans. They quickly focused on marriage, college and careers. However, for a few, there was now an irresistible attraction to "far-away places with strange-sounding names."

This was especially true of a West Texas rancher's son named Zack. He tried to settle back into the routines of feeding, branding and fence mending, but he turned every conversation to the little South Pacific island where he had heard natives talk about a mountain of diamonds.

"They're there for the takin'," he would say, "And someday I'm gonna go back and get 'em." I guess that's why nobody was surprised when one morning his old mother found his bed had not been slept in and his navy duffle bag was gone. Almost a year later, the parents' fears were confirmed when they received a letter mailed by boat from his talked-about island.

That was the last word they received. After two years of waiting, the family decided it was time for action. Most of the ranch's stock was sold at a poor price to finance the oldest boy's going in search of his brother. Another year had passed before his persistence was rewarded. Landing on a volcanic island fitting the description in his lost brother's letter, he was encouraged to find natives who spoke of a white man who had indeed come seeking sparkling stones. Many moons had now passed since he was last seen disappearing into the rain forest to ascend the steep path up the volcano.

Immediately, the new arrival announced his intention to rescue his lost brother. The natives were horrified and warned him not to repeat the foolishness of the other white man. They insisted that the man he sought was probably dead, because the only path up the mountain was constantly guarded by a stately lion. So many islanders had perished in the jaws of the beast that any attempt to trespass his territory had been abandoned. In living memory, only the fortune-seeking Texas cowboy had dared to face the danger. Now, the man who sought him was cautioned not to go on to certain death.

"I must go," he insisted. "Isn't there any way?"

An old sage stepped forward to say, "Perhaps." He went on to explain that the inhabitants of the island were worshipers of the Immortal Porpoise. If the determined brother would be willing to convert to their religion, perhaps the Immortal Porpoise would protect him from the stately lion. Reluctantly, the Baptist rescuer agreed to embrace the beliefs of the islanders. For a month, he was taught daily by the old wise man. Finally, at high tide under a full moon, he underwent his initiation in a torchlight ceremony on the beach. At first light the next morning, he walked into the jungle, determined to find his lost brother.

His climb up the steep mountain path was without incident with no sign of the lion. High on the volcano, near the crater, just above the tree line, he found a primitive mining operation and his baby brother, Zack. The once-hopeful diamond miner was almost beyond hope. His provisions were exhausted. His health was broken. His sanity was fragile. The jewels he sought were nowhere to be found. After a day and night of feeding and treating the failed miner, his brother decided to attempt a descent. With great effort, he balanced Zack across his shoulders, and carefully began picking his way down the path.

On slippery ground, deep in the rain forest, his worst fears became reality. There, asleep across the path, was the stately lion. Swallowing hard, he breathed a prayer to the Immortal Porpoise, stepped across the slumbering beast, and hastened on his way. Within an hour, he emerged from the jungle and was home free. Exultant, he rushed his ailing brother to the nearest village and told everyone what had happened.

His joy was short-lived. Within a week, he was arrested by the governor for that district of islands and charged with "transporting a miner across a stately lion for immortal porpoises."

A Horse of a Different Color

"**I** DIDN'T COME HERE TO HORSE AROUND." NOW there's a line you've never heard from the hero in a Western movie. A cowboy's horse is no joking matter. Most of the steeds I remember were heroes in their own rights.

Can you imagine Gene Autry without Champion, Roy Rogers without Trigger, Dale Evans without Buttermilk, The Lone Ranger without Silver, Tonto without Scout, Tom Mix without Tony, or Hopalong Cassidy without Topper? These trusty mounts were always just outside the jailhouse window, ready to stretch the rope attached to the saddlehorn and bars, freeing their unjustly held masters. They stood still while foolish heroes leaped into the saddles from second-story windows. They went for help when disaster struck, and horned in when a school marm tried to kiss the cowboy.

Without horses, our collection of cowboy songs would be mighty slim. Bob Wills rode his "pony on the reservation...in those Oklahoma hills." Gene Autry rode that "strawberry roan" into bronco-busting immortality. Roy Rogers waxed plumb romantic as he looked Trigger in the eyes and sang, "Old Faithful, we rode the range together; Old Faithful, in every kind of weather. When your round-up days are over, there'll be pastures white with clover for you, Old Faithful, pal of mine."

Old Paint went on from song to become the name of a thousand Pinto ponies. "Ghost riders in the sky" kept us on the straight and narrow with visions of lathered horses breathing fire.

As a boy, my favorite books were about horses: *Black Beauty, My Fiend Flicka, Thunderhead, Wildfire* and *Smoky, The Cowhorse.* They fired my imagination and brought broomsticks alive between my legs.

Of course, growing up in West Texas ranching country, I knew that while a cowboy and his horse were inseparable, the romance of fiction and the hard facts of reality didn't exactly coincide. I saw this illustrated in conflicting relationships between horses and a quiet, slow-talking, even-tempered cowboy named Stan. To be around him when just people were present, you would swear that nothing could rile him, but throw a horse into the mix, and trouble was brewing. One bitterly cold morning, a little blue stallion tossed its head as the cowboy swung into the saddle. Realizing that he'd just come within a hair's breadth of a broken nose, Stan smashed a gloved fist into the animal's skull. It sure was embarrassing explaining to folks at church the next Sunday how he broke his hand. I reckon that wasn't nearly as frustrating as the day that same ornery little horse threw Stan in a pasture two miles from the house. In a rage, he threw dirt clods at the critter until it disappeared over a rise, then had to walk home in high-heeled cowboy boots.

Horse trading probably gave rise to the saying, "Let the buyer beware."

Thinking he knew a good thing when he saw it and not being ashamed of taking advantage of a naive preacher, a cowboy in the canyon country of the Texas Panhandle bought a pretty young mare from an evangelist who was passing through. As they parted, the parson said, "Now, son, I've got to warn you, she won't take to no rough cowboy talk. She's been raised hearing me quote scripture, and she only responds to a good Christian vocabulary."

"Like what?" asked the cowboy.

"Well, for instance," said the preacher, "If you want her to move on out, you say 'praise the Lord.' If you want her to stop, you say 'amen.'"

A week later, with the preacher's warning dim in his memory, the cowboy was loping his new horse near the rim of the Palo Duro Canyon. Suddenly realizing that they were in a precarious situation, he pulled back on the reins and shouted, "Whoa!"

Taking the bit between her teeth, the mare dashed straight toward a 200-foot drop into the canyon. In the midst of a frenzied rehearsal of the horse's ancestry, the cowboy remembered the evangelist's instructions. "Amen!" he shouted. Seconds later, in a cloud of dust, the horse stood trembling on the very edge of the cliff. Weak with relief, the rider said, "Praise the Lord!"

Dirty Tricks

THERE IS A GOOD REASON THAT MEN WHO grew up on the farms and ranches and in the small towns of West Texas are not easily taken in by used car salesmen, get-rich-quick schemes and retirement property real estate offers. Early on they were victimized by a parade of extended family members, grinning brothers, older classmates and a collection of bored men looking for cheap amusement. Any Muleshoe kid who turned 16 without being cynical deserved his own chapter in "Gullible's Travels."

Perhaps the best-known illustration of this syndrome was from the "Peanuts" comic strip. Charlie Brown had a propensity for believing that Lucy would hold the football while he ran up to kick it. Of course, the little round-headed kid should have learned years ago that she would jerk the ball away at the last minute, and he would end up flat on his back.

My own education in this regard started with an uncle whom I much admired, but whom I learned to watch cautiously. He had served with the United States Navy in the South Pacific during World War II, and returned to my maternal grandparents' empty nest to work as an oil field roughneck. Looking at his and my father's forearms convinced me that getting a tattoo was surely part of the initiation into manhood. His collection of *True, Argosy* and *Esquire* magazines introduced me to the writing of Ernest Hemingway and to the exploits of racehorses such as Man o' War, Seabiscuit and Whirlaway. My strongest memories of him are of the Vargas Girl calendars on his bedroom wall and the way he would leave me hanging. On at least two occasions during my childhood, he coaxed me into letting him lift me to the top of a door frame. After encouraging me to get a good grip with my fingertips, he would turn me loose and walk away.

That should have taught me not to trust anyone, but a kid couldn't spend years hanging out around a county seat barber shop and not fall prey to a full array of other dirty tricks. On more than one occasion, I had one of my father's customers ask me to run down to the hardware store and see if they still had their sky hooks on sale. These were the same old geezers who delighted in asking small people with limited childhood vocabularies if that was a garment on their backs, or if they ever found "vittles" on their plates. It was enough to keep any nine-year-old boy looking over his shoulder in every mirror and developing a very finicky appetite.

A lot of grown men wasted good pocket change on hot summer afternoons. They delighted in gluing dimes to downtown sidewalks, then gleefully watching from inside a store as a boy would try to casually pick them up without anyone noticing.

One of my most embarrassing memories is of the infamous nickel-funneling episode. The guys who hung out around the Phillips 66 filling station, on Muleshoe's Main Street, lay in wait for naive boys like a coyote watching for a jack rabbit. You knew they were up to no good, but they were the most believable liars in Texas. I knew this, but I was still drawn in by a grease monkey's shout of "Hey, I'll bet you can't do this!"

There I was, in a circle of grinning cowboys, mechanics and loafing high school football players. The guy who had set the trap held an oil funnel in one hand and a buffalo nickel in the other. "Here's how it works," he said. "You stick this funnel into the front of your pants, tilt your head 'way back and let me put this nickel on your forehead. Then, if you can slowly bring your head down and make the nickel drop into the funnel, I'll give you a 50-cent piece."

Sizing up the funnel, I thought that it looked big enough to drop such a small coin into, and 50¢ was enough for a movie ticket, a box of popcorn and money left over for a cherry Coke® and a funny book. In no time at all, I was concentrating on not letting the nickel miss its mark and counting my chickens before they had hatched. The shock of a quart of cold water being poured into the funnel caused my head to snap forward and sent the nickel flying all the way into the middle of Main Street. For the rest of the afternoon, I flinched through explanations to my smiling father and my shoe shine customers about how my pants got so wet.

It didn't take too many such experiences to cause every boy to long for the day when he could get even by wreaking the same havoc on a tender junior member of the human race. One of the most popular West Texas outlets for this vengeance was to find a kid longing for acceptance and take him snipe hunting.

While being driven out into the country by a knowledgeable group of older boys, the anxious novice would hear the snipe described as a furry, harmless animal that is about the size of a skunk. He would be told that snipes don't see well, and that they always run in a straight line when they are frightened, making them easy to catch. At last, he would be positioned in a dark place with a burlap sack and told, "Wait here. We'll go up there a ways, scare one up and run him back toward you. Get in his way, and he'll run right into your sack."

Many a town boy has been left holding the bag in the middle of a ranch pasture on a cold, dark night while his country cousins whooped and hollered miles away. By morning, he had probably already decided on some younger victim that he wanted to take snipe hunting. Thus, the cycle continued.

Such childhood training resulted in a bunch of teenage boys that were hard to fool and spoiling for trouble. A Bailey County watermelon farmer learned this the hard way. Exasperated by the constant overnight loss of his choicest melons, he posted a sign on the edge of his field which read, "One of these watermelons has been poisoned." He was amazed the next morning to find the handiwork of some local scoundrels who had been led down the yellow brick road one time too many. His sign had been altered to read, "Two of these watermelons have been poisoned."

Say What?

OVER A SUNDAY LUNCH, A WEST TEXAS farm family was discussing the morning services at Longview Baptist Church. "What did you learn in Sunday School today?" Deacon Baldwin asked seven-year-old Skipper.

"Well," the boy stated, while pushing green vegetables around with his fork, "We learned about how Moses got the children of Israel out of Egypt."

"How did he do it?" asked his mother.

"It was really neat," said Skipper. "They came to this big lake and the Egyptian army was right behind them, so Moses had his corps of engineers float pontoon bridges. He got all his infantry, tanks and supply trucks across, then he called in the Israeli Air Force to strafe and bomb. They sank the bridges, and all the Egyptian soldiers were either shot or drowned."

Incredulous, the flabbergasted father asked, "Skipper, is that what Mrs. Killingsworth taught you?"

"No, sir," the boy replied, "But if I told you what she said, you wouldn't believe me."

So it is that out of the misunderstandings, imaginations and the honesty of children come some of the most amazing things.

Four-year-old Tommy liked to lead in blessing the food before family meals, but he had developed a habit that taxed the patience of his parents and siblings. He would peek between his fingers and ask God's blessing on each article of food on the table. The topper came during a visit by his mother's parents. Being careful not to overlook anything, he prayed, "God, bless the peas, the carrots, the meatloaf, the bread, the mashed potatoes and the..." Framed between two of his fingers, Tommy saw his grandfather's face. "And bless Paw Paw; he's so ugly."

While growing up in Muleshoe, I had a neighborhood friend who had an especially overactive imagination. One day he spotted a big shaggy dog loping across his backyard. "Mom, Mom!" he yelled. "There's a real live bear in our yard!"

After checking on the intruder, the concerned mother said, "Randy, you've got to stop exaggerating. That's not a bear; it's just a big dog. Now, I want you to go to your room and ask God to forgive you for fibbing to me."

Some time later, a chastened Randy walked back into his mother's kitchen. "Did you do what I told you to do?" she asked.

"Yes," the boy replied. "But God said it was okay. He said that the first time He saw that dog, He thought it was a bear, too."

He was the same kid who begged to go back to church on Sunday night because he thought he had heard the pastor announce that they would be ordaining some new "demons."

There's something about a pastor's visit that seems to put even upright folks on edge. Add the presence of a child, and most parents start acting like a cat on a hot tin roof. Sister Mary Neal was already uptight over entertaining Rev. Filbert when six-year-old Buddy dashed in with a wild-eyed look on his face. Not seeing the preacher, he blurted out, "Mother, I was in the garage and I saw this mouse, so I smashed him with Daddy's shovel. Then I stepped on his head. Then I picked him up by the tail and threw him against the wall. And then..."

Finally, Buddy had spotted the startled pastor. Putting on his best Sunday School face, the boy folded his hands and quietly said, "Then, Mother, God called him home."

Men, Boys and Toys

A LONG TIME AGO, A WISE MAN CONCLUDED that the difference between men and boys is the price of their toys. Any wife can tell you that the boy never goes away inside of a man. Here I am into my seventh decade and, when no one is looking, I will put on dark glasses and a baseball cap, sneak off to a mall and spend an hour browsing in a toy store.

Every time I see a box of Cracker Jack® on a store shelf, I am overwhelmed with a desire to buy, not for the caramel popcorn, but for the toy inside. Is it still there?

It is a great disappointment that you can no longer cut the top off of a cereal box, wrap a quarter in tissue paper, mail these to Battle Creek, Michigan, and get all kinds of neat stuff in return. Oh, what I would give to still have my ranger badges that glowed in the dark, or my rings with siren whistles, compasses or secret compartments.

Toys have always reflected the times when they were made. Today, Barbie wears a "power suit" and is running for president, turtles wear masks and deliver karate chops, games are played on video screens instead of boards, and guns shoot rays instead of bullets.

During the '40s and '50s in West Texas, every farm and town kid's toy chest held a mix of store-bought and homemade toys. Until my eleventh birthday, when I left the playgrounds of backyards, alleys and vacant lots for the work of shining shoes in Daddy's barber shop, my annual accumulation of toys was pretty predictable. Christmas brought the big haul, and the want list was made up after hours of poring over the Sears and Roebuck and Montgomery Ward catalogs. Birthdays usually meant books. This was okay, but it called for creative acquisitions at other times. Summer vacations with my maternal grandparents offered the best opportunities. Mother's occasional shopping trips to Clovis and Lubbock also raised my hopes of satisfying some childhood lust for possession.

Today, television and websites fuel the greed of small minds. Fifty years ago, my strongest desires were ignited by Saturday afternoon "shoot-'em-ups" at the Valley Theater. I just had to have Gene Autry double holsters with simulated pearl-handled pistols. Red Ryder was both a comic book and movie hero. This meant that my proudest possession was a Daisy® Red Ryder lever-action BB rifle.

Some articles of clothing or equipment, associated with my matinee heroes, were frustrating when it came to buying or duplicating. I could never find a black scarf exactly like the one which the Durango Kid used for a mask, and no one was willing to let a little kid have a bullwhip like the one used by Lash LaRue.

My grandfather, Sam King, was my supplier of toys that fired my imagination and took on great value. I have absolutely no musical talent, but he bought me several jew's-harps and harmonicas. These instruments had provided him countless hours of entertainment as a young West Texas cowboy. I treasured them and tested my grandmother's nerves by discordant twanging and blowing.

My mother put my BB gun and the slingshots, which my grandfather manufactured, in the same category. If I heard her say it once, I heard her say it a thousand times, "You're going to shoot somebody's eye out."

Some toys were the products of the cooperative work of the kids from a whole neighborhood. How many hands that would later build bridges and skyscrapers must have gotten their early training digging forts and building tree houses? One of our block's best joint ventures was the barrel that was rigged with ropes and suspended between two Chinese elm trees. After it had been padded with some mother's cast-off blanket, it made a great place to test your manhood while pretending that you were riding a wild bull or bucking bronco. Of course, the experience was always made more harrowing by our buddies' gleefully jerking on the ropes.

Show me a grown man's obsession today, and I will have a pretty good idea about his favorite toys as a kid. For instance, a guy who likes to swat a little white ball around 40 acres of grass is probably the boy you remember kicking a tin can all the way home from school.

Some men never get over being completely controlled by their toys. Their sense of values is taken to ridiculous extremes. This was true of the yuppie who wrecked his new car. The first person to arrive at the scene of the accident found the dazed driver standing at the edge of a cliff, watching his vehicle burn in the ravine below. The poor man seemed oblivious to the fact that his left arm had been severed. He was wailing, "My new BMW! I've lost my new BMW!"

"Are you crazy?" asked his rescuer. "Don't worry about your car. Just be thankful that you're alive. Right now we have to get you some help. You've lost your left arm."

"My left arm!" screamed the victim. "Oh, no, my Rolex! I've lost my new Rolex, too!"

Maybe this is why the best toys are not the ones that cost the most money, but the ones that exist primarily in our imaginations. Don't resent it when you

see a child more interested in the box than the expensive product it contained.

The Box

The big ole box surely was made
To hold grand and expensive stuff.
On the heap of wrapping and ribbons it would've stayed,
'Cause that Christmas he had more than enough.
But it caught the eye of the daring young spy,
Whose deeds were many, secret and brave.
He needed speed-of-light transport o'er land, sea and sky,
And the box was everything a six-year-old boy could crave.

School Days

SOME SONGS GET STUCK IN YOUR MIND forever. For me, these include "My Adobe Hacienda," "You Are My Sunshine," "Frankie and Johnny" and "School Days."

The latter started with, "School days, school days, dear old golden rule days; reading, and writing and 'rithmetic taught to the tune of a hickory stick." That sounds pretty abusive and archaic in light of today's progressive, outcome-based education; but it worked for the majority of the folks who built the United States into a world leader.

I'll always be grateful for a succession of Muleshoe public school teachers who were consistently firm and caring. They were always addressed as "Mister," "Miss" or "Missus," even when any of them were met long after graduation. I still felt compelled to say, "Sir" and "Ma'am." I was reminded of this when I returned to Muleshoe for the first time in 30 years and saw Mrs.

Watson. I remembered it again when I heard of the death of Mrs. Blackburn. I count myself among the blessed ones who were taught in the first grade by Mrs. Mary DeShazo, for whom a Muleshoe elementary school is now named.

I'll always remember Superintendent Jerry Kirk with great respect, even though he called me "Rex." The confusion was caused by his memory of a former student whose last name, "Briscoe," was too close to my own.

All I have to do is let my mind slip into neutral, and it is flooded with memories from school days: drawing plans for rocket ships during English class; feeling compelled to add my name to those of students who previously carved their monikers onto my third grade desk; being encouraged to keep writing when I showed Mrs. Smiley my fourth grade attempt at a Western novel; fingers stained by a leaking fountain pen; sneaking wax paper out of Mother's kitchen to speed my descent on a slide during recess; the pleasure of getting a big pile of Valentine cards; coloring stenciled turkeys and autumn leaves with crayons so they could decorate a classroom wall; being frustrated because the kid who sat in front of me in the fifth grade could wiggle his ears and I couldn't; hunting Easter eggs on the courthouse lawn; and school being dismissed so that we could see a matinee showing of *Lassie Come Home.*

Elementary school taught me that perfection would always elude me in accomplishing some tasks. For instance, even though I followed instructions to the letter, I could never keep from making a mess of those book covers provided by local merchants. They always turned out like my Vacation Bible School projects. While other kids made complicated bird houses, I had to be satisfied with bookends, which consisted of two sanded and varnished blocks of wood. The varnish was never smooth.

Once I got to college, I was even more grateful for the elementary and high school teachers who refused to give me an easy ride. Without them, I would not have survived my freshman year. "Easy come, easy go" has taken on all-too-graphic meaning for many talented, but undisciplined, possessors of high school diplomas.

This was true of a good ole boy named Pete, who had bluffed and coasted through 12 years of school before landing on the Texas Tech campus. After bouncing off the brick walls of a few required math and English courses, he went looking for an easy passing grade. While devouring a hamburger in the student union, he overheard some upper classmen talking about an old, tenured professor who taught a class on ornithology. He had no idea what that meant, but he was immediately interested when he heard someone say, "All you have to do is show up, and he will give you a passing grade."

Sure that he had found an easy way to improve his grade average, Pete signed up to study birds. Unknown to him, that same day the old professor decided to retire. In his place, the university hired a bright-eyed, gung-ho, young teacher who was just out of graduate school. Obsessed with birds, he expected the same interest and commitment from his students. From the first day in the class, Pete knew that he was in big trouble. The fatal blow fell the day that the young professor sprang a pop quiz. "Your performance on this test will determine 50% of your final grade for this course," he announced to a stunned class.

He proceeded to pass out sheets of paper containing pictures of 25 varieties of bird legs.

The smiling teacher said, "You have 15 minutes to correctly label each set of legs."

Exasperated, Pete crumpled the test page in his hand, gathered his books and stood to leave. "Just a minute," said the professor. "What's your name, young man?"

Stopping in the doorway, Pete pulled his pants up to his knees and said, "You tell me, sir."

The Only Good Snake

A S A BOY, I WAS ALWAYS TOLD THAT "THE only good snake is a dead snake," and nothing in my personal experience has done much to disprove that. I will admit to surviving a few unlikely close encounters with cold-blooded, scaly creatures, such as posing for a picture beside a road in India while struggling to keep a python from wrapping me in its muscular coils. I've also watched the pro-reptile *National Geographic* videos and specials on the Discovery Channel, but snakes still give me the creeps.

Blame it on the environment. Growing up in West Texas isn't conducive to becoming a snake lover. There are just too many rattlesnakes, and the best public relations company in the world couldn't clean up their image.

Everybody I knew in Muleshoe and Bailey County had his or her own horror story about a diamondback.

These ranged from amazing to tragic. The most amazing concerned my Uncle Bishop's old shepherd dog. As a puppy, he came out on the losing end after attacking a rattlesnake, but lived to see his master off to World War II, welcome him home to the family farm, and was still around when I entered my teen years. In dog years, he was over 100. That snake must have made him immune to everything.

All the kids in my neighborhood had a daily reminder that the strike of a rattler usually spells tragedy. The toughest member of our gang had to cope with a hand deformed by a snake bite. My brother, Dudley, made it through his West Texas childhood unscathed, but then stepped on an Oklahoma rattler. For the next year, his immune system was in a shambles.

Knowing the consequences of being surprised by a rattlesnake caused all of us kids to walk with a special alertness, and to watch with apprehension every time a favorite dog or horse would dash into high weeds. If you wanted to make a friend jump a mile high, all you had to do was yell, "Snake!"

Before I was ten years old, I had watched my mother kill a dozen rattlers in our yard with a garden hoe. I was also aware of the neighboring housewife who inexplicably found a five-foot-long critter coiled in her bathtub. I think I tried to skip at least one Saturday ritual after that.

This obsession with poisonous reptiles made it pretty hard to believe a grandfather or uncle when he pointed to a bull snake and said, "Those things are good to have around. They won't hurt you, and they keep mice out of the chicken feed." Sure, they weren't going to hurt me, but that didn't mean they wouldn't make me hurt myself.

This "good snake" business was sure never bought by my Auntie Ethel. Just bring them up in a conversation, and she would leave the room. Her phobia helped create one of the most memorable evenings of my childhood. My maternal grandfather, Sam King, had herded everybody in his house to the storm cellar as a threatening cloud loomed over Jones County. As we huddled in the damp earthen dugout with pickled beets and canned peaches, somebody with the good sense to keep quiet spotted a slick, black snake on the ledge over the only door. The rest of the evening was spent keeping Auntie from seeing this threat to her sanity. By the time the thunderclaps had receded to a distant rumble, we were all masters of distraction.

Everybody I know is afraid of snakes, but for some reason it's not manly to admit it. I've seen many men appear cool and blasé while struggling to conceal a cold sweat. Some have pushed this crazy test of manhood to the unlikely sport of rattlesnake hunting. Sweetwater, Texas, has turned this into their biggest annual event. I'm still convinced, however, that the bravest man is just a split-second away from giving any snake his house or ranch.

One of our good friends recently had her opportunity to prove that I'm right. Discovering a rattlesnake in the front yard of their ranch house, she placed an emergency call to her husband who was in California on a business trip. His unconcerned reaction was, "Why are you bothering me? It's no big deal. Take care of it."

Infuriated by his lack of empathy, she turned her wrath on the hapless reptile and "took care of" him. The heat of her anger, however, was still directed toward her husband. She decided that getting mad was not enough; she would look for a chance to get even.

A couple of days later, her husband was back at work on the ranch. When she left the house to take a sack lunch and a jar of iced tea to where he was baling hay, she knew that opportunity was knocking. She fetched the dead snake from the weeds where she had left it. A few minutes later, she parked her Jeep beside their old blue pickup and observed her husband hard at work on the far side of the field. She lovingly placed his lunch and tea on the seat of the truck, then she carefully coiled the remains of the rattler on the floorboard between the brake and the gas pedal. When her husband reluctantly tells the story, he says that he was just about to take his first sip of iced tea when the toe of his right boot nudged the snake. The next thing he recalls is being flat on his face about ten feet from the pickup, clutching an empty jar. For about the next hour, the dead serpent owned that pickup.

He knows how to sympathize with the West Texas farmers and ranchers who met up with a snake-handling evangelist from the mountains east of the Mississippi River. The preacher had decided to go west and do missionary work for his particular cult. Any hope of his getting a Bailey County following was shot to pieces on the first night he managed to coax a few bewildered and curious folks into a little one-room church house near a rural cotton gin. Things started downhill when he pulled a handful of squirming rattlers from a burlap bag and dropped one. Making a break for freedom, the snake slithered in the general direction of the congregation.

Pandemonium broke out. It was worse than the Mississippi squirrel revival. Women stood on the tops of pews, lifting their skirts and screaming. Old, arthritic men were leaping over benches. The befuddled preacher was simultaneously trying to quell the storm and count his snakes. In panic, a cowboy knocked a church deacon down and asked, "Where's the back door to this fool place?"

"We ain't got one," he was told.

In wild-eyed desperation, the spooked ranch hand asked, "Well, then, just where have you always wanted to have one?"

Never Too Old

AFTER FORMER PRESIDENT GEORGE BUSH, at the age of 72, flipped backward from an airplane and plunged 8,000 feet in a free fall before opening his parachute over the Arizona desert, he said, "It was wonderful. I'm a new man."

Add this Yale University baseball player, World War II bomber pilot and world leader to a long list of senior citizens who have done more starting than stopping. The cover story about Bush's accomplishment in the March 26, 1997, issue of *USA Today*, also cited 90-year-old grandmothers who are earning their black belts in karate, beautiful and sexy Sophia Loren, in her middle sixties, and Lena Horne, better than ever at the age of 80. Tony Bennett made a comeback that landed him on MTV, and Pat Boone raised eyebrows with a heavy metal CD. No one seemed surprised when Story Musgrave flew as an astronaut in the space shuttle at the age of 61, or when John Glenn went back into space at the age of 77.

For years, I've talked to crowds of teenagers about "Making Sense Out of Sex." Now, I'm considering a seminar for folks who are 55 and available. I'll probably call it, "Everything You Need To Know About Dating You Learned in the Eighth Grade." When my wife, Robbie, and I make our frequent visits to Arizona, we find that "Falling in Love Again" could be the theme song for Sun City. Now that's as scary as skydiving!

Of course, all this reverse aging isn't really anything new; it's just that more folks are getting in on it. There have always been "never say die" achievers who have dared to spit in the face of time. Colonel Harland Sanders could look back on more than 60 years when he finally figured out the right combination of all those spices. Harry Truman had lived long enough to fail utterly as a businessman before he laughed at the premature headline that declared Dewey a winner in the 1948 presidential election. Benjamin Franklin had been a newspaper columnist at the age of 16, but at 81, he was still around to help frame our constitution. George Bernard Shaw was 94 when one of his plays was first produced. Golda Meir had already retired as an American schoolteacher when she became the prime minister of Israel at the age of 71.

My grandfather, Sam King, had a heart attack when he was in his late 50s. When a doctor told him to retire, it made him mad. He decided to "refire." At the age of 81, he sat down in his porch swing and closed the book on a full life of cowboying and preaching.

My wife and I had the privilege of knowing Dr. Clifford B. Jones, for whom the football stadium at Texas Tech University is named. During his latter years, Robbie was his secretary. During his lifetime, he experienced Colorado in its pioneer robustness, was a manager of the Spur Ranch in West Texas, president of Texas Tech, chairman of the Board for Lubbock National Bank and a long-time member of the board of directors for the Burlington Railroad. He declared that he would never retire because he had seen that kill too many of his friends. He came to the office on time every day until he was 87.

A wise man said, "It's what you do, not when you do it. Age has nothing to do with dreams and determination."

If this trend toward total living by people who are 55 and better continues, young people may begin looking to role models who have silver instead of orange hair. If this happens, we really can look to the future with hope. This won't come easy, because in our society, respect is hard to come by. The popular creed seems to be, "It's okay if I get in your face, as long as you get out of my way."

Generation Next had better be careful. Old Satchel Paige said, "Don't ever look back; somebody might be gaining on you."

When today's seniors look back, however, they realize that they're the ones who are gaining ground. We are the fastest growing age group in North America, and we're not easily pushed around. If you don't believe that, you need to talk to a wiser teenager who tangled with an elderly West Texas widow in the parking lot of Lubbock's South Plains Mall. The brash young man gunned his sports car around the little grandmother's big car and scooted into the last choice parking place. The infuriated woman lowered a car window and shouted, "You can't do that!"

Flipping his keys into the air and catching them, the grinning punk said, "Yes, I can, because I'm young and quick."

He was almost into the mall when he heard a crash and the grinding of metal. Looking back at the parking lot, he was horrified to see that the widow had plowed her Cadillac into the back of his little yellow convertible. The sports car was now wedged between the big sedan and the massive bumper of an oversized pickup. Racing up to the demolition, he screamed, "You can't do that!"

Smiling sweetly, the lady said, "Yes, I can. I'm old and I'm rich."

Susie's Funeral

BACK IN THE EARLY '50S, BAPTIST REVIV-
als were still newsworthy and local radio stations often welcomed visiting evangelists to
share early-morning programming with farm news,
country music and funeral announcements. A Louisiana preacher had just had his 15 minutes on a 500-
watt county seat station to promote the spring meeting
at a West Texas church. When he and the pastor returned to the parsonage for a breakfast of ham and
eggs, the local parson's wife was talking on the phone.
Stretching out the receiver to the visiting preacher,
she said, "It's for you. Someone who just heard you on
the radio."

"Hello," said the evangelist.

"Howdy, preacher. I'm glad I caught ya. This here's
Joe Bob Gibbs. I've got a ranch out east of town a
piece. Me and the wife heard ya this mornin'. I told 'er,

'That man's a real human bein'. Yes, sir, a real human bein'. I believe he's the one that can help us.'"

"Thank you," said the preacher. "How can I help you?"

"Well, preacher," he heard. "I hate ta admit it but I ain't much of a churchgoin' man. I don't know many men of tha cloth, and now we need one real bad."

He wasn't sure, but the evangelist thought he heard a break in the voice that sounded like it belonged on the sound track of a Hollywood Western. "I'll help if I can. Tell me what's happened," he said.

"It's Susie," said the caller. "She's been a part of our family for 20 years, then last night she jest up an' died. I told the wife that we can't jest bury her, but I don't know no preachers or nothin'. Then we heard ya an' I said, 'That's the man that can help us. He's a real human bein'.'"

"I'm sorry about Susie," said the evangelist. "Have you thought about when and where you want to have the funeral?"

"I reckon we don't have no choice," said the rancher. "It'll hafta be out here. Could ya do it this afternoon?"

"Hang on for a minute," said the evangelist. "I'll be right back."

Laying the phone down, he asked the pastor, "Do you know Joe Bob Gibbs?"

Surprised, the pastor said, "Everybody around here does, but not too many preachers would know him real well. He's got a reputation for being tough and ornery. What's this all about?"

"Somebody in his family has died, and he's looking for a preacher to help with a funeral this afternoon. He wants me to do it."

"Tell him yes," insisted the pastor. "This is a great open door!"

"Mr. Gibbs, I'll be glad to help," said the visiting preacher. "Tell me how to get to your place, and we'll come on out as soon as possible."

Twelve miles east of town on a farm-to-market pavement, the pastor turned left and crossed a cattle guard under a wrought-iron arch. A horizontal "G" was centered on the arch. In the space on either side, the evangelist read "The Lazy G Ranch." For another two miles, they followed a gravel road bound by barbed wire fences. Flat pastures stretched away to the heat waves on a pale blue horizon. Quality quarterhorses and fat Hereford cattle grazed amid prickly pear cactus and mesquite trees. White dust billowed behind the pastor's Chevy.

A white house with a wraparound porch sat in the shade of big Chinese elm trees. Behind it were a gray weathered barn and corrals. A windmill turned slowly, its pump creaking as cold water gushed into a moss-covered tank

Susie's funeral had drawn quite a crowd. Pickup trucks, Cadillacs and four-wheel drive vehicles were parked everywhere. Women talked on the porch. Children chased each other around the house, up the trees and over the fences. The evangelist's attention was caught by the cluster of men under the largest tree. Everyone wore a hat. Some of the hats were straw, some black, some gray, all big. From the bottom, boots were the dress of the day. The heels couldn't be seen because everyone had bought his jeans six inches too long.

As the pastor and the evangelist hesitantly climbed out of their dust-covered car, an old man stepped away from the group and strode toward them. His belt buckle looked like a big shield. His dirty gray hat had been repeatedly hand curled on the sides until it came to a point over his eyes. He was bowlegged and looked to be a lot taller from the belt buckle up. His white hair and sun-baked skin were like silver against the leather on a Mexican saddle. His pale blue eyes were reddened and moist.

"Preacher, thank ya fer comin'," said the old rancher. "Like I told the wife, yer a real human bein'."

"I'm glad I can help," said the evangelist. "This is my pastor this week. I wanted him to come along."

"Howdy," said their host. "Thanks fer bringin' this here preacher. He's a real human bein'."

Walking toward the house with Joe Bob Gibbs, the evangelist brought up the thing that interested him most. "Tell me about Susie," he said.

"Well," said the old man. "Like I said, she's been a part of our family fer 20 years. Why, all of our kids learned to ride on her."

Joe Bob kept talking, but the man who was there to preach Susie's funeral didn't hear him. Stunned, he let the truth sink in. "Good grief," he thought. "Susie wasn't a real human being; she was a horse!"

Still in a daze, the evangelist found himself in the parlor of the house surrounded by intently watching ranch folks. Across the room, the pastor squeezed into a corner. He was very pale and very quiet.

"Before we go to the grave side, could ya sang my favorite hymn?" asked the rancher.

"I'll try," said the Louisiana preacher. "What is it?"

"The Last Roundup," said the old man.

By now the pastor was either deeply in prayer or about to burst into laughter. His face was buried in his hands.

Suddenly thankful for those many hours of singing to himself while driving from one revival meeting to another, the evangelist surprised himself and broke into song. When he finished, grown men were blowing their noses, women were hugging each other and children were bawling. The pastor was out on the porch.

The evangelist was thinking, "Singing preachers are like dancing dogs. Neither one's very good at it, but it's a lot of fun to watch them try."

"Well, it's time," said the rancher, reminding the reluctant preacher of what they always say at midnight to condemned men in grade-B movies.

The party moved into the yard where six cowboys leaned on shovels near a huge mound of dirt. For the first time, the evangelist was aware of something covered by a large canvas tarp. It was on the opposite side of a big hole from the cowboys and the dirt pile.

When a circle had formed around all of this, the rancher solemnly nodded at the evangelist. What followed was a mishmash of God's expressing His love toward us by giving us animals, and His understanding our grief when they're taken away, and a strong, "Amen."

The tearful old man nodded again, and the cowboys moved around to jerk the tarp off the body of a brown-and-white paint mare. She was stiff as a poker. Sobbing broke loose as the hired hands manned poles under the carcass and strained against the dead weight. With a crash that shook the yard, Susie slid into her final resting place.

"That's it. Let's go," said the flustered pastor. He half-pushed and half-dragged the dazed evangelist toward the car. The motor was already running when Joe Bob put his hand on the passenger's door.

"Preacher, I can't ever thank ya enuff," said the shaken rancher. "Like I said, yer a real human bein' and I want ya ta have this."

Halfway back to town, the evangelist decided the pastor wasn't going to talk, so he opened the envelope Susie's grief-stricken owner had given him. He looked at the check and was stunned as he read the amount— $1,000!

"Pastor, I'm through preaching revivals. From now on, I'm burying horses."

To Tell the Truth

I F ANY GRANDCHILD TOLD THE TRUTH, HE OR she would have to admit that half the fun of visiting grandparents is that you can get away with twice as much. That's probably because memaws and pepaws know that they can give the little tykes what they don't need and then send them home before they turn green. My mother always declared, "If I had known that grandchildren would be so much fun, I would've had them first."

As a boy, I looked forward to the June day when I could climb on a train or bus in Muleshoe and make the trip to my maternal grandparents' Jones County home. For the next six weeks, I would be allowed to sleep until 10:00 every morning, drink at least three Dr. Peppers every day (at 10, 2 and 4), eat tons of fried chicken, fried okra, rolls made from scratch, rich lemon pie and great angel food cakes, and put half a cup of sugar into one glass of iced tea. I could go with my grandmother to buy chicken feed and pick out the designs for a couple of new shirts that would be made from the sacks before I returned home. My grandfather would make sure that I got a new straw hat, and I could forget about shirts and shoes, except for the trips to town on Saturdays and to church on Sunday.

"Spoiled" is defined as "blighted" and "deteriorated." Most mothers will agree that it doesn't take long with Grandma for a son's or daughter's attitude to be blighted or for their behavior to deteriorate. It was always a rude awakening to come back under my mother's regime after a summer of "getting away with murder."

Of course, even a grandparent can be pushed too far. A few of these "enough is enough" episodes come to mind. Leaving the gate open and letting the milk cow into the garden wasn't a good idea. Collecting all those glass eggs from the hens' nests could push an easy-going grandmother over the edge. Even a preacher grandfather could be provoked to an expanded vocabulary when someone wore his best work gloves while making mud pies. He sure enough forgot all the scriptures about forgiveness when three dominoes came up missing from his favorite set.

When it comes to "take your life in your own hands" missteps, two take the cake. The first was brought on by the fact that, for some reason which I never understood, the lock was on the outside of the outhouse door. I reckoned this perhaps had something to do with keeping unwelcome critters out.

It was inevitable that temptation would overtake me on a hot July afternoon when I had too much time on my hands. My poor grandmother, who never did anything to deserve something like this, became a prisoner when I tripped the wooden latch on my way to the barn. I must have been exploring among old harnesses and antique hardware for the better part of an hour when her screams finally caused me to realize that I was dangling from the horns of a dilemma. There was no one else on the place to take the blame, and I had provoked her into a rage that I didn't know was possible. Could I move fast enough to flip the lock and disappear before my world came to an end? I tried, but I couldn't.

Thankfully, the worst out-of-bounds grandchild adventure happened to my summertime buddy, Ralph. That time, I was able to learn from observation instead of experience.

Just about every rural home in Jones County had a cistern to catch rain water. This was a precious commodity and it was rigorously protected. The worst possible offense was to leave the lid off the cistern. With the weird assortment of creepy crawlies abounding in West Texas, there's no telling what a startled grandpa might find in his dipper.

Poor Ralph had the misfortune of forgetting to cover his grandfather's cistern on the same day that an old tomcat disappeared. When one occurrence proved to be related to the other, fear quickly spread through the house. Somebody was in big trouble, and judgment was coming. Ralph was spared immediate destruction by the presence of about six other grand-children and four or five of us neighbor brats. For the next hour, the place reverberated with declarations of "It wasn't me," and "I don't know who did it."

Finally, Grandpa Bailey said, "That's it! I'm gonna get my truth brick."

A puzzled cluster of kids watched him return to where we stood near the back porch. I was asking myself, "What in the world is a truth brick?"

We were all instructed to stand in a circle, and Ralph's grandfather took his place in the middle. "Now," he said. "Since none of you seems willing to 'fess up, I'll let this here truth brick nail the culprit. Here's the way it works: I'll toss this thing into the air and it'll come down square on the guilty person. Okay, get ready! Here she goes!"

Before the brick ever left his grandfather's hand, Ralph was doubled up in fear, clasping his hands over his head. After that, before I tried anything on any-body, I wanted to be double sure that they didn't have a truth brick.

Pedal Power

EVERY NOW AND THEN, SOMEBODY COMES up with the germ of a good idea, then another guy perfects it and, after a while, somebody else can't leave well enough alone and messes up the whole thing. In my opinion, that's exactly the history of the bicycle.

In 1790, a guy in France made a wooden scooter that was about as practical as handlebars on a park bench. A few other fellows in Scotland and Germany had a go at it, until in about 1885, an Englishman named Starley put his "safety bicycle" on the road, and the world was into pedal power.

By 1890, folks were pumping along on bikes with air-filled rubber wheels, coaster brakes and adjustable handlebars. The bicycle now existed in its simplest, most solid form. For the next 80 years, this would do just fine for millions of people in Europe, Asia, throughout the Americas and in Africa. During the war years (1939-1945), thousands of people in the United States found cars, gasoline and tires to be in short supply, so they turned to the bicycle. My mother had one with a small front wheel and a large basket. She used it to haul groceries, laundry and an occasional small boy.

These practical coaster models were the bikes of my youth. I look at the high-priced, gear-loaded, only-a-genius-can-work-on-them, yuppy toys of today, and I long to be able to get my hands on another Schwinn Flyer®. That was the bicycle of all bicycles. It had a headlight, rear fender reflector, carrier for school books or a buddy, leather streamers at the ends of the handlebar grips, a chain cover, padded seat and a neat encasing below the top tube.

In spite of all this luxury, any ten-year-old boy could learn the basics of mechanics by working on his own bike. Some of my proudest moments were when I had successfully fixed a flat, oiled a chain, adjusted a seat or tightened handlebars. A dog and a bicycle went a long way in teaching a kid the meaning of responsibility. Everybody I knew had a bicycle. None of my town friends ever had to ask a parent to take him or her to the swimming pool, ballfield or to the store. Anywhere a kid wanted to go was just a quick ride away.

Bicycles also fired the imagination. What boy didn't lust after a motorcycle? While that possibility was still just a distant dream, you could always sneak the joker out of a deck of cards, snatch a clothespin off your mother's backyard line, clip the card to a fender support and cause housewives to rush to their front doors to check out the strange motorized vehicle that was thumping down their street.

How many boys and girls have ridden their bicycles into their first experience in the American work place? Multitudes of households have depended on a neighbor kid and his bicycle to insure the arrival of the morning paper. My bike gave me a good excuse to hang out at the local Santa Fe depot to deliver telegrams to grain elevators, lawyers and banks. I lived for the afternoon when one would arrive for the not-too-successful retailer who hit the sauce right after lunch every day. If he received a wire about 3:00, his tip was unbelievable.

What I like least about the newfangled bicycles is the braking system. Having to use two hands to ride is a bummer. It makes it impossible to take a dog along while holding his lead with one hand, and it assures that most modern kids will never become really good at riding all over town without touching the handle-bars.

A bicycle allowed me some of my best times alone as a boy. When I needed to get away, I could just climb on my bike and take off. I did a lot of thinking while coasting with the West Texas wind at my back. Often, when things get a little hectic, I remember summer afternoons when I would straddle my bike on the west side of Muleshoe and watch a sunset until twilight. Every boy needs wheels.

Young West Texas bikers grew strong pedaling into the wind, but they grew spoiled into believing that all ground is flat and that they should always be able to see for three miles ahead. I guess that's why a not-too-swift lad from the South Plains got so confused when his folks sent him off to summer camp in the wooded mountains of New Mexico. During the first week, he got separated from his group during a biking run in an area that was especially thick with brush. Looking for a shortcut, he got off the trail into the chaparral and had a flat tire.

The search party had already been organized when the bedraggled camper pushed his bike out of the woods from the opposite direction from where he was expected. "Why did you take the long way out?" asked the concerned camp director.

"Well," explained the boy. "My bike was pointed that way, and it's easier to push in there than it is to pull."

Electric Sky and Dry Land

WHEN I WAS IN THE FOURTH GRADE, I read J. Frank Dobie's book, *The Longhorns*. I still remember his chapter on "stompedes." He used the old Texan word that captured perfectly the consequences of spooking a herd of nervous Longhorn cattle. He pointed out that the word used was a corruption of the Spanish word "estampida." An old cowboy described it by saying, "It's one jump to their feet and another jump into hell."

Dobie declared that nothing else had the potential to ignite a stampede as did a thunderstorm. He illustrated this by quoting Walt Cousins' poem, "The Stampede":

Lightnin' rolls in hoops and circles,
Rain in sheets is comin' down,
Thunder rattles through the gulches,
As the hoof-beats shake the ground.

Top hands ride like likkered Injuns,
Beggin' God for the break o' day.
A stampede beats the best camp meetin'
When it comes to gettin' men to pray.

When I first read those words, I could understand the terror provoked by the fury of a monster storm sweeping across the plains. From my earliest childhood in West Texas, I had known that nothing else combined the power, uncertainty and threat of a night exploding with thunder, lightning, wind, hail and slashing rain. In my poem, "Llano Estacado," I wrote about "hail from an electric sky, and crashing thunder that just won't die."

My awe, fear and respect for a thunderstorm were born out of hearing my grandmother talk about the time she had been caught up in a tornado. No one else that I have met has survived such an ordeal. Her night of terror resulted in her being found in a field a quarter of a mile from a destroyed house, covered with debris.

This experience resulted in not one, but two, storm cellars on my grandparents' Jones County property. In the days before storm chasers, Doppler radar and TV alerts, my grandfather began a constant vigil whenever he heard the first rumble of thunder. As soon as he decided that this looked like a bad one, everyone was out of the house and underground to spend the night inhaling the smell of damp earth and listening to the clatter of hail on the tin door.

Storm watching is easier on the South Plains of West Texas than it is in places where trees and hills shorten the horizons. In Bailey County, you can stand in a farm yard and watch a streak of lightening from the clouds to the ground 30 miles away.

As a boy, I remember one particular summer of intensely studying thunderheads. It was the summer that I learned to swim and desired to spend the bulk of every afternoon in Muleshoe's public pool. Two things could interfere with my daily plunge. One was my mother's rule that I could not go into the water until one hour after eating lunch. The other was the threat of rain. Nobody was allowed in the water if thunder was rumbling. No one that I knew was acquainted with anyone who had been struck by lightning and was still walking around and talking about it.

Just as soon as lunch was over every day that summer, I would check the time and put a towel and my swim trunks into the basket of my bicycle. For the balance of the hour, I would study the sky. Thunderheads usually started building during the early hours of a July or August afternoon. If I so much as glimpsed a cloud the size of my fist, I would try to will it away. No one has ever exercised the power of positive thinking as much as I did that summer. In spite of this, I saw many modest cumulus clouds build and mount until they towered 40,000 feet over the South Plains.

If I saw any darkness, heard any rumble or if I saw a streak of lightning, I would keep my fingers crossed, make every effort to keep my mother in the house and pray that she had seen or heard nothing.

It is hardly possible for me to disconnect my childhood memories of rain from violent thunderstorms. It was only when I married and moved my family from Lubbock, Texas, to Richmond, Virginia, that I fully realized what a regional phenomena this is. We still laugh about the day our adolescent son was watching a gentle rain fall from a Virginia sky and said, "Look! The rain just falls straight down here."

Because rain was so tied to those rampaging storms, it was a matter for both prayer and dread. For a West Texas dryland cotton farmer, rain at the right time was a matter of survival.

The problem was that it often proved to be a matter of destruction. One devastating afternoon of hail could lay waste to months of plowing, planting, cultivating and hoping.

West Texas was and still is a land of weather extremes. "Drought" was a word heard early and often, but "flood" was also in the vocabulary of farmers and ranchers. One cloudburst could fill every buffalo wallow between Littlefield and Friona and turn dry stream beds into raging torrents of brown water. If the moisture from a Gulf Coast hurricane decided to camp out over the South Plains for a few days, prairie dogs and jack rabbits had better know how to swim. During the springs of 1942 and 1957, high water closed the roads out of Muleshoe in every direction. In '57 it was said that a few farmers used boats to get to town so they could cash their drought-relief checks. Of course, these were unusual extremes; and the years that separated such occurrences gave plenty of time for memory to be seasoned by imagination. Actually, any significant amount of rain in the West Texas of my youth brought such blessing or destruction that it was not soon forgotten.

When the rains failed, West Texas farmers and ranchers were not hesitant to turn to prayer. This is not to say that these were super-pious people, with a pipeline to Heaven. My father used to laugh with his barber shop customers about the folks that went to church to pray for rain and got soaked going home because they hadn't carried umbrellas. One of my favorite stories is from the legendary exploits of the cowboy preacher, B. B. Crimm. He traveled by horseback and was followed by a pack of hound dogs. When he preached in rural churches, those dogs would sleep around the pulpit. He was every inch a man's man. Cowboys who wouldn't give a "panty-waisted preacher" the time of day, stood still and listened when Crimm talked.

One long, hot summer, pastures on the high plains were drying up and the bottoms of stock tanks had turned to patches of hard, cracked earth. Desperate ranchers had called on this man of God to pray for rain. On an appointed day, he rode out to meet a delegation of area stockmen. Sitting on his horse in the shadow of a windmill, he asked, "How many of you men tithe?"

There was considerable hawking, spitting and boot shuffling, but nobody answered in the affirmative. "Hmmm," said the preacher, swinging out of the saddle. Kneeling down, with a hand in a stirrup, he prayed that it wouldn't rain for three years, mounted and rode away.

Man, The Hunter

I F IT IS TRUE THAT HUNTING IS AN INSTINCT born into man from his creation, the inclination was sorely tested when he decided to settle on the Llano Estacado, the Staked Plains, above the Texas Caprock. Unless you're into eating critters such as badgers, polecats, prairie dogs, jack rabbits and coyotes, that boundless sea of grass doesn't afford much game. The prairie chickens and buffalo that sustained the Comanche Indians were wiped out as fast as the white men's guns could manage. That pretty well narrowed the choice down to birds on the wing.

As a boy, I didn't do much hunting, because I was a town boy and the scarcity of suitable game. Of course, the latter didn't stop those fellows who had killing bred into them like a thoroughbred has running bred into it. Hanging around my father's barber shop, I heard them spin many tales about stalking and sniping.

A few old-timers skated on the edge of credibility, like the farmer who swore that during the hardest days of the Great Depression, they had to make sure they didn't waste any jack rabbits. He said that he and his little brother had the job of running alongside the bounding bunnies and feeling their sides to see if they were fat enough to eat.

Birds did keep the wolf away from many pioneer doors. There were quail, pheasant and doves on a pretty steady basis; and a couple of times a year, geese and ducks slowed on their trips north and south to invade the grain fields of West Texas. As a little boy, I thought that duck meat just naturally contained buckshot, like a catfish has bones.

One fowl, the Sand Hill crane, was a no-no for hunting as far back as I can remember.

Every autumn, huge flocks of these magnificent birds arrived to spend winter on the alkali lakes southwest of Muleshoe. Early every morning and late every afternoon, they would darken the sky as they rose from and returned to Coyote Lake.

If one was just into pulling triggers and watching fur fly, without eating being a consideration, critter-hunting was plentiful. Some fellows even supplemented their income by ridding ranch pastures of coyotes.

Most West Texas boys end up doing their share of hunting jack rabbits. Just about any night you can find four or five guys with .22s trying to freeze the long-eared creatures in the headlights of a pickup.

During one of my few forays into jack rabbit hunting, I thought I had played the fool one time too many. A buddy was driving a pickup at breakneck speed across a ranch pasture in pursuit of our zigzagging prey. Three of us brave predators were in the pickup bed with guns. Too late, the crazed driver saw an approaching fire ditch. He slammed on the brakes just as the bumper plowed into a ridge of earth. Before I could think, I was airborne with a rifle in my right hand. As I looked down on the bed of the truck, I thought, "I hope somebody's gun doesn't go off." As it turned out, the guns were the least of my worries. My right shin came down on the lip of a feed can. For the next month, I tried to think up a good story that would allow me to blame my limp on something really heroic.

A lot of barber shop regulars took vicarious satisfaction in hearing the yarns of the few flatlanders who ventured into the Rocky Mountains each fall to hunt elk and deer. Every now and then, somebody who had grown up back east would entertain us with his memories of 'coon hunting. It wasn't the stories about the 'coon hunters, but the ones about their dogs that really fascinated me. The exploits of these special dogs took on mystical proportions as they were told again and again.

My favorite 'coon dog story had to do with the guy who went to one of the top breeders in northwest Alabama, looking to buy a champion. He was pointed to a young black and tan who showed unusual potential. "I reckon he's gonna be one o' tha best ever," boasted the seller.

"Sure 'nuff," sneered the skeptical buyer. "How'm I gonna know that?"

"Well," said the dog's grinning owner, "You jest tell me how big a 'coon you're hankerin' fer, an' he'll fetch it whiles you wait."

Holding his hands about two feet apart, the prospective buyer said, "One 'bout that long would be jest fine."

Stepping into his workshop, the breeder sawed off a two-foot plank of wood and showed it to the dog. Immediately the hound wheeled and dashed into the woods. Within 30 minutes he was back with a 'coon exactly two feet long.

"If he can do that again, I'm sold," said the impressed customer. "Have him get one this big," he said, holding his hands a foot apart.

After being shown a foot-long plank, the dog was off to the hunt. This time, in less than 15 minutes, he was back with a foot-long 'coon.

"Wow! That's fer sure tha most amazin' thang I ever seen," said the hunter. "Here's a hunderd dollars down. Hang onto 'im and I'll be back Saturday to pay ya off and pick 'im up."

On Saturday afternoon, the excited buyer drove up with a new hound cage in the back of his pickup. "Bring 'im out and I'll load 'im up," he said.

"I sure wish I could," the breeder said, "but we ain't seen that crazy hound since a little after you left here the other day."

"What happened?" asked the concerned hunter.

"Well, I ain't rightly sure," said the owner, "but my wife propped her ironing board up out here on tha porch, an' that fool dog took one look and took off."

Off to a Good Start

NO OTHER MEAL GETS TALKED ABOUT AS much as breakfast. Think about it. Who can't remember his mother asking, "Did you eat your breakfast?" How many times have you been told, "Breakfast is the most important meal of the day"? It seemed that all of my school teachers had to repeat the advice, "Breakfast like a king, lunch like a prince, and dinner like a pauper."

In spite of this, it's hard to come to a real agreement on just what makes a good breakfast. I'm personally aware of tastes that differ from a sister-in-law who prefers chocolate cake and Coca-Cola® to my own leaning toward classic cholesterol-chart busters.

Vitamins, powdered mixes and fruit-flavored snack bars have just about destroyed a proper appreciation for breakfast. A person must be older than blenders, microwave ovens and rush-hour commuting to have really good breakfast memories.

My earliest morning meals included having my father crumble toast into my over-easy eggs, so that they wouldn't look yucky, while he spun yarns about breakfast when he was a boy. Oatmeal was big even then. It never made any sense to me, but his best memories were not about the slimy globs of steaming gook ladled out to his mother's brood. They were of her making the leftover mess into flat cakes that became after-school favorites. The appeal of this never captured my imagination.

By the time I was old enough to express strongly my own breakfast preferences, I shared the common lot of every American child since the invention of comic books and radio. My choices were dictated by advertising. If Tom Mix was sponsored by Ralston®, that had to be my cereal. If Bob Feller's picture was on a box of Wheaties®, "the breakfast of champions," there had better be a supply in our cabinet, even if the taste was bland. I'm not sure Ovaltine® ever did anything to improve my health, but its manufacturer's backing of Little Orphan Annie and Captain Midnight caused me to do a lot to add to their wealth.

Without a big Kellogg's® or Post® cereal box always being propped in front of me at the breakfast table, I would probably have ended up in a remedial reading class. I spent a lot more time studying the virtues of corn flakes than I did pondering why Dick wanted to see Spot run.

Monday through Friday at our house was dominated by cereal, hot or cold, sliced banana, milk, toast and jelly. Weekends were something else. On Saturdays, after staying in bed long enough to hear a few of my favorite kids' radio programs, the certainty of pancakes would draw me to the kitchen. This got even better after my father gave my mother a waffle iron as a Christmas present. She may have preferred something else, but it suited my brother and me just fine.

Sundays were the days which set in concrete my thinking about what it takes to make a real breakfast. While my father, brother and I crowded onto the living room couch with the funny papers, Mother was busy stirring cream gravy, frying strips of bacon, making biscuits from scratch and frying eggs. To this day, I can endure raisin bran or instant oatmeal on any weekday morning because I know that Sunday is coming.

Of course, today's stand-ins for the real things include canned low-fat biscuits, all-vegetable-protein breakfast patties, no-cholesterol egg substitute, no-fat powdered gravy mix, fake butter, decaffeinated instant coffee and skim milk. My taste buds have been fooled so many times they don't trust anyone.

When I hear a man say, "I don't eat breakfast," I immediately look on him with suspicion. He probably doesn't like dogs or fruitcake either. He may not have watched *Casablanca* or *Miracle On 34th Street* more than once. I'll bet he goes to work without reading "Blondie" or "Dick Tracy." It's likely he doesn't have a favorite sweater that's more than 30 years old. Is this really the kind of person with whom you would entrust America's economy or government? A croissant and a cup of coffee may be okay to begin a day in San Francisco. A bagel with cream cheese may be good enough in New York, but it still takes more in America's heartland.

This tradition is not just guarded at farm and ranch tables from Minnesota to Texas, it is preserved in hundreds of small-town coffee shops. These keepers of the breakfast flame are found on main streets and beside state highways in places such as Friona, Littlefield, Dimmitt and Muleshoe. Beginning at 5 a.m., they are easily spotted by the collection of muddy pickups and company vans clustered around them. No one with any "smarts" will try to mingle with the regulars without a hat or baseball cap sporting an agribusiness promotion. A request for a no-smoking section or an order of decaf coffee marks a person as an outsider for sure. In these places, the mingled smells of smoke, strong coffee and bacon-and-egg-flavored grease hang heavy. Here you find the last outposts of breakfast like it was meant to be: real butter, heaps of grits, biscuits made for soakin' syrup and soppin' gravy, sugar-cured ham or crisp bacon, eggs fried over-easy, short stacks of pancakes that are thick in the middle and greasy and crisp on the edges and coffee that will wire you 'til lunch, all served up by a waitress who knew what you wanted before you asked for it and who doesn't take any sass.

Of course, these good ole boys learned how to eat breakfast at their mamas' tables. You can still find this kind of home cooking if you show up early enough at a West Texas farmhouse. A full and happy visitor from back East had just discovered this as the morning guest of a Bailey County family. Standing on the porch with his host, he remarked that he had never eaten better ham. About that time, a three-legged pig made its way from the barn toward the house. Pointing to it, the visitor said, "Now, that's sure interesting."

"Yep," said the farmer. "That there is some pig. In fact, our family owes it a lot."

"How's that?" asked the curious city slicker.

"Well," said his host. "First of all, we would've burned up in our house if that porker hadn't set up such a fuss that he roused us in the nick of time. Then, 'bout a year later, he pulled our youngest boy out o' the stock tank and kept him from drownin'."

"Wow! That's great!" proclaimed the visitor. "Did he lose that leg in some heroic act?"

"Nope," said the farmer. "But when you've got a pig that's done that much for you, you can't just jump up and eat 'im for breakfast all at once."

Eatin' Just For Fun

EATIN' USED TO BE FUN,
'Til the food police came around.
They nixed the good stuff one by one,
Fearin' we'd enjoy a bite or gain a pound.

Once chocolate was a pure delight.
Snickers®, Hershey's® and Baby Ruth® were all the best.
Now one small mint is a cause for fright.
Sneaking an m&m® is a sin to be confessed.

All-vegetable meat subs don't fill the bill.
Give that to those mean diet-imposing brutes.
I'll take whole hog 'til I've had my fill,
Shunnin' what's made from leaves, twigs and roots.

These assassins of the palate
Have no country to which they hold.
Mexican and Chinese get "no" on their ballot.
Why, even Southern Fried makes them scold.

It's high time to put the food bullies in their place.
Let's insist on beef and cake 'til we've had enuff.
Bring on French pastries with sugar lace.
Dump tofu for buttered rolls, fat ribs and stuff.

I'm ready to find the pound I lost.
I'm tired of readin' an' doin' math 'fore I eat.
Faced with pie, must I count the cost,
Or eat it quick, before the meat?

Sure, life's short, so let's have some fun.
Immoral and illegal go too far,
So good eatin' must be the one.
Messin with that's a cause for war!

Lie Down and Be Counted

FINALLY, A CHAMPION FOR A REALLY GREAT cause! Someone has written a book about the importance of napping. He suggests that those of us who have always known the value of a good nap should "lie down and be counted."

Isn't it strange that we seem to begin life resisting any attempt to get us to take a midday snooze, and then spend the rest of our existence trying to sneak a nap into our mad rush through life? If you think about it, you'll see how natural napping is to the healthy flow of things. Why do we seem to believe that our bodies and minds are up to no good, and that they have to be jerked back into line, just because they cry out for a little shut-eye after lunch?

This "don't get caught napping" mentality isn't natural; it's learned. It all started when Thomas Edison invented the electric light bulb, then lied about not needing much sleep. He was really an all-time world-class champion cat-napper. He hit us going both ways with a double-edged sword. He made it possible for us to stay up all night working or watching television, and then he sold us all that baloney about sleep being bad.

Let's get this thing straight once and for all. Is napping a bad thing? Well, let me ask you if you trust your dog. Sure you do. Then observe him. You'll never find No-Doz® stocked next to Alpo®. Do you trust your grandfather? Sure you do. Then observe him. Sit him down in front of a television set, and, bingo! It's lights out in no time at all.

We have enough to feel guilty about without adding napping to the list. Why get stressed out over one of the best things God ever designed to relieve stress? Fighting the urge to nap turns decent people into bald-faced liars. How many businessmen do you think are really working behind those closed doors when they tell their secretaries they're not to be disturbed between 2:00 and 3:00 every afternoon? As a young pastor, one woman in my church could turn me into a blithering fount of denial by beginning every telephone conversation with the question, "Did I wake you up?"

Only in North America and the European countries north of the Alps is napping frowned on. I was delighted when I went to Portugal and discovered that, even in the major cities of Porto and Lisbon, businessmen close offices and shops for two-hour lunches, followed by good naps.

When someone obsessed with making every minute count tries to make you feel guilty about catching 40 winks between appointments, remind them that high-octane accomplishers such as Albert Einstein and Bob Hope credited their ability to take frequent short naps for their ability to do so much for so long.

Sometimes the smartest thing a boss or teacher could say would be, "Let's all take a break and get a good nap." Would such an attitude bring America to her knees? I say no, based on my best examples. My maternal grandparents worked hard. They put in long days. They survived by growing and preserving their own fruits and vegetables, while raising chickens to eat and lay eggs, milking a cow, fattening calves and hogs, making lye soap, churning butter and curing meat. I remember two things about their sleep patterns. They were early to bed and early to rise, and they took a nap after lunch every day. I can still see, in my mind's eye, my grandfather stretched out on his back on the front porch with his sweat-stained straw hat keeping flies off his face. Twenty minutes later, he would be off to brave the afternoon heat.

Sure, I can remember when I thought it was child abuse for my mother to make me waste perfectly good time taking an afternoon nap. Even when I didn't sleep, those enforced siestas became times when I could sort things out in my mind. It was while lying flat of my back and puzzling over plaster designs on ceilings that my imagination expanded. I nurtured daydreams, which blossomed into ambitions. I'm glad that someone smarter than I was insisted on my being still for a little while every day.

Of course, there will always be those busybodies who waste good time bugging sleepy people, when they themselves could be taking a nap. I was nodding off in my shine chair on a hot July afternoon when a cowboy stumbled into my father's barber shop and fell victim to the sleep police. The poor guy had been up since before daylight. He had herded a bunch of surly cattle to Muleshoe's railroad loading chutes and was looking for a place to crash and burn. A vacant shop bench seemed to be just what the doctor ordered.

It would have been if his rolled-back eyes, lolling head and open mouth had not proved too great a temptation for a couple of the shop's regular loafers. Everybody leaned forward with anticipation as a grinning tormentor gently stuck a loose piece of cigarette paper to the sleeping cowboy's bottom lip. When he expelled his next breath, the paper fluttered like a crazed insect, and the startled object of perverted amusement just about beat his own head off. Without a word, he jerked his hat down over his eyes and stormed out to the accompaniment of hoots and hollers.

It's about time some people were told that they can act busy if they want to, but the rest of us are going to take a nap. If they're smart, they'll let sleeping dogs lie.

Just Holler

WILL ROGERS SAID THAT HE NEVER MET a man he didn't like. My father always said that this was because he never had an opportunity to introduce the cowboy philosopher to a few folks he knew too well.

While I have met my share of soreheads, the greatest delight of being able to travel the world for the past umpteen years has been getting to know many good and interesting people. Solidly entrenched on my top-ten list is Ermon Godwin, Jr., the mayor of Spivey's Corner, North Carolina. When this Southern gentleman retired from the banking business, he was just getting started. Today he is known internationally as the founder, promoter and president of the National Hollerin' Contest.

Not only has the hollerin' contest put the little crossroads community of Spivey's Corner on the map, it has also preserved and given due attention to a great

American tradition. A while back, driving me to the Raleigh/Durham airport, Mr.Godwin brought me up to speed on the practice's origins and variations.

Hollerin' is both a means of communication and a way of getting someone's attention. Actually, the contest at Spivey's Corner is broken into three categories. There's honest-to-goodness hollerin', then there's whistlin', and conch shell and foxhorn blowin'. I guess it boils down to using whatever you've got handy to get the job done.

Obviously, hollerin' was a necessity for folks before telephones, fax machines and email made it possible to reach out and touch someone, especially right in the middle of dinner every night. Mr. Godwin described good hollerin' as the same as humming, but being able to be heard more than a mile away. A thesaurus will tell you that it's related to bellowing, calling, crying, screaming, shouting, shrieking or yelling.

While the tradition has been enshrined in the sandy farmlands of North Carolina, it's been practiced anywhere there was somebody with a good set of lungs and a need to send a message. Men at sea have made "Ship ahoy!" one of history's most familiar hollers. Like other all-out cries, this one often has some real urgency attached to it. This was the case on a foggy night when a navy watchman spotted what he assumed was a light on a ship in his vessel's path. Alarmed, he shouted, "Alter your course immediately!"

Through the fog came the reply, "No—alter your course immediately."

"Comply now!" screamed the sailor. "You're talking to a battleship!"

"No, you comply," came the cry in the night. "You're talking to a lighthouse!"

For years, during the days of the old Southwest Conference, football fans across Texas had their nerves rubbed raw by the hog callin' of those rude folks from the Arkansas hills. Of course, these Razorback boosters were just doing the kind of hollerin' that their ancestors had found both natural and necessary. A hoarse fellow in Pine Ridge might have been told by Lum or Abner that he sounded like he'd been calling fat hogs up a steep cliff. As long as there are pigs to be fed, some young farm boy will be learning to yell, "Whoo pig, sooey!"

West Texas cowboys might have learned their hollerin' style from the Comanche warriors who preceded them in taming mustangs and roaming the Llano Estacado. These ranch hands had their wild whoops tamed and made melodic by songs such as "Whoopee-Ti-Yi-Yo" and "I'm an Old Cowhand," and Eddy Arnold's rendition of "The Cattle Call." Even today, a leanin' tall drink o' water, who will get tongue tied saying "Howdy" to a pretty girl, has no compunction about hollerin' loud enough to scare small children when he's trying to move a stubborn cow out of the corner of the corral.

As Jerry Clower taught us, sometimes a good ole boy just feels better lettin' loose with a big whoop. The next time things build up to the bustin' point on the inside, let off some steam by rarin' back and lettin' go with a primitive male holler. That ought to get your wife's and kids' undivided attention for a couple of days. It sure helped Tarzan keep Jane and all those apes in line.

When we were talking about the National Hollerin' Contest, I forgot to ask Mr. Godwin if they allow women to enter. Come to think about it, that might not be fair because, as we all know, mothers are natural born hollerin' champions. When I was a boy, it always amazed me that the same mother who had told me so often that it was not polite to yell at people would stand in our back door and shout my name loud enough to be heard by half the town. Her first couple of hollers usually went unheeded, but when her calls of "Wayne" were expanded to "Clinton Wayne Bristow!" I knew it was time to respond posthaste. I always had great empathy with the radio series character, Henry Aldrich.

About two dozen grandkids and cousins would be playing at grandma's house, and they would all ignore the clanging of the dinner bell. Things changed when she stood on the back porch, put her hands on her hips and hollered, "If you don't come and get it, I'm gonna throw it out!" That triggered an all-out stampede for the dinner table. Anybody who stubbed his toe and fell down knew that he might as well just lie there and play in the dirt; it was too late to get anything to eat.

Probably more folks have hollered for help than for any other reason. As all mothers know, children get lots of practice at doing this. Maybe that's why they take such pleasure at bellowing their kids' names throughout the neighborhood. They're just gettin' even.

My buddy, Steve Shirk, embarrasses his oldest son, Joseph, by recalling how he combined hollerin' with his potty training. Taking on babysitting responsibilities while his wife, Betty Jo, was shopping, Steve parked Joseph on his potty just as the telephone rang. Soon Daddy was involved in an important business conversation, and the trainee was stranded in an awkward position. Before long, Steve's phone negotiations were interrupted by a pleading call of "Daddy!"

"Daddy's talking on the phone, Joseph. I'll be there in a little while," he shouted.

After all of this was repeated three times, Steve asked his party to hang on while he took care of an emergency. Entering the bathroom, he said, "Joseph, I'm in the middle of an important phone call. What do you want?"

In his most pitiful voice, Joseph said, "I just want to know how old I'm going to be when you come back to help me."

Driving with the Windows Down

RECENTLY, NEEDING TO PICK UP SOMEthing at a neighborhood shopping center, I backed our car out of the driveway and drove two blocks before I realized that I had not raised the windows and turned on the air conditioning. Talking to myself, I remarked, "Hey; I'd forgotten just how good this feels!"

That started me to thinking about what driving was like in the days before power steering, automatic transmissions and air conditioning. Today's kids know all about a baseball or basketball player coming through in the clutch, but they would be totally discombobulated if they looked down and saw an extra pedal in the floorboard of the family car. That means we have two or three generations on our hands that don't know anything about "speed shiftin'" or "layin' rubber."

During the '40s and '50s, driving courses hadn't found their way into high school curricula. Back then, it was a daddy's responsibility to take his son or daughter out on a deserted country road and teach the art of going from first to second gear without the car going through a spasm of leaps and stops. That was always the acid test of any parent-child relationship.

While today's teenage drivers might view their fingers as being needed primarily for tuning the stereo tape player, my 1950s-and-earlier bunch learned a whole series of hand signals. Of course, not everybody was quick to catch on. One high school cheerleader was pulled over by a Bailey County sheriff's deputy because she had turned left while signaling to turn right. Her defense was, "Oh, shucks. I was just dryin' my fingernail polish."

Maybe it was just because I grew up on the South Plains of West Texas, where there's absolutely nothing to interfere with airwaves, but it seems that car radios were more powerful in the '50s than they are now. While cruising Main Street in Clovis, New Mexico, on a hot summer night, we could pick up music from New Orleans to Los Angeles. My wanderlust was nurtured while surfing radio frequencies in a Ford Fairlane.

Don't get me wrong. Not everything about pre-computerized vehicles was glamorous. Ask anybody older than a baby boomer if he has any good childhood memories of cramming everybody into the family car for a summer trip. A couple of hours of blowing hair, sweat-soaked clothes and frayed tempers were more than enough motivation for somebody to get busy and invent automobile air conditioning.

I'll never forget the first air-conditioned car I ever saw. I had this great-uncle out in Globe, Arizona. Every summer, he and his wife would spend his vacation from the copper mines driving back to Texas to visit kinfolks. One blazing hot July afternoon, when everybody was trying to find some shade and relief, here came Uncle Ira and Aunt Annie driving up in a shiny new Buick with all the windows rolled up. They climbed out cool as cucumbers with not a drop of sweat in sight. For the next hour, we took turns letting Uncle Ira drive us around and demonstrate the contraption that allowed a fan to blow cold air off a chest full of ice. I figured they probably got in about a hundred miles between ice houses.

After they went home, my grandfather nearly suffocated driving around town with the windows of his Pontiac coupe rolled up. He didn't want anybody to think his brother-in-law had anything he didn't have.

It wasn't long after that incident that a Bailey County farm boy was trying to hitch a ride out on the Lubbock highway. A Dallas lawyer, in an air-conditioned Cadillac, screeched to a stop.

"Where you goin'?" he asked.

"I'm headin' over to Lubbock to see the circus," the boy replied.

Opening the passenger door, the city shyster said, "Climb in. I'll take you all the way there."

They hadn't gone two miles before the rider rubbed his blue arms and said, "Mister, I reckon you can let me out 'bout right here."

"Son, I thought you said you was goin' to Lubbock," said the lawyer.

"Yes, sir, I was," the boy explained. "But since it's up and turned off cold like this, I think I'd better go back home and help Daddy kill hogs."

From the time Americans started puttering across county lines in Model Ts, our country has been getting smaller and smaller. Now, with 70-mile-per-hour speed limits, four-lane interstate highways and space-age cars, cross cultural communication is as common as hitching up a buggy was for our great-grandparents.

Recently, a seven-year-old beneficiary of modern automobile travel wandered away from his parents at a West Texas truck stop. Bug-eyed, he stared at a lean, sun-baked bowlegged man who was paying for gasoline. "Mister," asked the boy. "Are you a cowboy?"

"Yep, I reckon I am," the grinning stranger replied. "See this here hat of mine? It's a sure 'nuff cowboy hat. It's big to keep the sun an' rain off my head."

Not convinced, the boy asked, "Are you really a cowboy?"

"Why, sure I am, son," he was told. "See this here big belt buckle? I won that ridin' bulls in Amarillo last year."

Trying hard to get his point across, the ranch hand said, "See this bandanna tied around my neck? Only real cowboys wear these. They keep the sun off our necks, and we can pull 'em up to keep dust out of our mouths and noses."

Frowning, the skeptical boy asked again, "Are you really a cowboy?"

"Yes, I'm a cowboy," declared the exasperated Texan. "Why won't you believe me?"

Pointing at the man's feet, the boy said, "Because you're wearin' them rubber flip-flops."

"Oh, those," laughed the cowboy. "I just wear 'em so folks won't think I'm a truck driver."

Go Take a Walk

RECENTLY, I READ THAT MORE SCIENTIFIC discoveries have been made in the last 50 years than in the prior 500 years. However, as I listen to the young whippersnappers who pass themselves off as modern health-and-fitness gurus, I'm convinced that a whole lot of what is being called a modern discovery is as old as the common sense of our great-grandparents.

For instance, look how long it took today's yuppies to discover what I heard my daddy say a thousand times, "You've got to walk before you can run."

Jim Fixx and Frank Shorter had us out sprinting through the 1970s and '80s in marathons and 5K road races. Only after our knees and backs had been jarred into early retirement did somebody "discover" that a good, brisk walk provides all the needed health benefits, not to mention allowing you to appreciate the passing scenery.

Now walking, the oldest and most natural way of getting from spot A to spot B, is being subjected to the same madness as jogging and running. There are magazines and books on walking. For proper walking, you must have a pair of especially designed $100 shoes. For several thousand dollars, you can take a walking vacation at a spa, where an expert will coach you on how to do what you thought you learned before kindergarten, put one foot in front of the other. For a few dollars more, you can be sent back home knowing how to look ridiculous strutting around your neighborhood, pumping your arms in an unnatural position and doing what is smugly called "power walking." Of course, to do it right, you'll need an overpriced set of miniature barbells and a pair of stretch pants that were sadistically designed by somebody jealous of anyone with a well-padded bottom.

There was a time when a guy would take a long walk in order to get a little peace and quiet. Forget that. In a time when the teenager nine cars in front of you at a red light loosens the fillings in your teeth with the volume of his stereo bass, you don't dare take the chance of going a few minutes without bombarding yourself with sound. No fear; a Walkman® tape or CD player takes care of your auditory input needs while walking. To be sure that you don't march to your own drummer, there are dozens of overgrown, still hyperactive young "instructors" ready for you to call their 800 number. Using your credit card, you can order a

$90 set of tapes that will make sure your pace and heart rate match their determined standard. Never mind that you'll be oblivious to the rampaging terrier that is closing in on your ankle or the pizza delivery car with which you're about share a quiet intersection.

When I was growing up in Muleshoe, Texas, anybody brash enough to try to pawn himself off as a walking instructor would have been laughed out of town. Everybody in my family walked everywhere: to work, to school, to the picture show, to the grocery store, to football games, to church and to visit friends. I can remember going to the corner, half a block from our house, and watching for Daddy as he walked home from work. I would rush to meet him (my first encounter with jogging) and walk the last two blocks with him.

My childhood walks had special rituals built into them. Any tin can or cardboard box that might cross my path had to be kicked all the way to my destination. Often a rock received the same attention. This explained the constantly scruffy toes of my shoes. No kid that I knew would have ever dared to step on the crack in a sidewalk. Some unwritten code seemed to threaten terrible consequences for anyone guilty of this infraction. It was almost as required that you skip through the moves of any hopscotch game chalked on concrete. Of course, the fact that these boxes were usually the artwork of girls caused us guys to take them a little less seriously.

Walking has always had its role models. During the newsreels, between features at the Valley Theater, we watched President Harry Truman jauntily strolling the streets of our nation's capital on his daily constitutionals.

Benefits from walking were also recognized before the modern craze. I remember a couple who were celebrating their 60th wedding anniversary. When a young reporter from the *Muleshoe Journal* asked the husband how he explained his remarkable health and long marriage, the old farmer smiled and said, "Well, when we got married, we agreed that if we had any arguments, we'd jest let whoever lost go out and take a long walk. I reckon I must've spent purt' near the last 60 years outdoors walkin'."

Now, a lot of us senior citizens are going back to what helped get us to where we are in pretty good health. Every morning, city malls are full of "50-and-better" walkers. It behooves us to keep using the common sense that served our forefathers so well. Of course, anyone can overdo a good thing, like the grandmother who decided to take up walking on her gerontologist's advice. He recommended that she walk three miles each day. She started off six months ago and her family has no idea where she might be today.

Sweat, Sand and Watermelons

MY GRANDFATHER USED TO DESCRIBE A blazing summer day in West Texas as being "as hot as a firecracker on the Fourth of July." I knew what he meant. If the day was 104° in the shade, if firecrackers popped all day and Roman candles lit up the night, if there was an abundance of homemade ice cream, fried chicken and corn on the cob, I always assumed that it was the Fourth of July.

You'll notice that I didn't mention a picnic. Now don't get me wrong. I'm about as patriotic as they come, but as far as I'm concerned, most picnics are a poor idea gone bad. The ones I've had a part in got worse before they got better. I decided early on that there must be a better way to celebrate the signing of our Declaration of Independence from our English cousins.

Picnics started back before air conditioning, when summer heat drove folks to seek relief beside a lake and under a shade tree. At least, that's how I always saw them pictured on calendars and in my mother's *Good Housekeeping* magazines. The problem was that around where I grew up in West Texas, we were sorely lacking both lakes and shade trees. At what passed for parks, the July sun had little trouble finding its way through the branches of a few scattered Chinese elm trees.

Another thing that complicated picnics around Muleshoe was that you could pretty well count on any chosen day's being blessed with winds from 25 to 35 miles per hour. That did aid digestion by putting plenty of grit into your craw. Sure enough, just when you thought that you had found a spot sufficiently protected from the gale, you'd discover that you were standing in the middle of a red ant bed. That's about as close as we Baptists ever came to taking dancing lessons.

One more thing about Fourth of July picnics turned me off. They were usually graced by a collection of my California cousins. I remember these towheads as being about as welcome to my brother and me as head lice and chigger bites. We knew that summer meant they were surely on their way to Texas. We also knew that they'd be there by the Fourth, but somehow their exact arrival was always a predictable surprise. The predictable part was that they'd drive up in the wee hours of the morning. The surprise was being shaken out of a sound sleep. In our two-bedroom, one-bath house there were just so many beds to go around. You guessed it—we ended up on the floor on pallets and the kinfolks got our beds. Because of them, it took me years to come anywhere close to having a good attitude about California.

On a few occasions, these summer picnics turned into full-scale family reunions. This meant having your cheeks pinched all day by gushing ladies who vaguely resembled someone you had seen in old photographs at your grandmother's house. The day always ended with me having the strange feeling that a lot of folks had been showing up and eating our grub who had no blood relationship with anybody on either side of our clan.

Around Muleshoe, with picnic sites being hard to come by, more often than not we headed for Horse-shoe Bend. This was a crescent, 100-foot-high san-dhill located in the middle of a ranch pasture. Because there wasn't a tree within 15 miles of the place, these shindigs were always late-afternoon-and-into-the-evening affairs. The food mainstays were roasted wieners, flaming marshmallows and watermelon. It was always the blessing of the night to be real sweaty from playing tag, and then to get soaked in melon juice and rolled down a sand hill. When it was time to load up and head for home, I knew what it would feel like to be a breaded piece of catfish. For days afterward, we'd find sand in the most amazing places.

None of these drawbacks ever dampened the enthusiasm for picnics among my family and friends, and never being one to pass on either ice cream or watermelon, I always showed up. After all, there was always the possibility of an unadvertized but unforgettable occurrence marking the event. This is exactly what happened when some mischievous cowboys spiked the watermelons for a West Texas Fourth of July celebration. After the town fathers had scraped out all the meat, the rinds were collected for preserves by members of the Homemakers Club. The ladies of the Garden Club were still around after dark picking up seeds.

Letting Grow

ONE CAN NEVER BET ON ITS BEING around to see the first freeze, but several times during July, I've started growing a mustache. I just can't let go of a childish compulsion to seek summer amusement. As a boy, I always had goals that were meant to endure only from early June until late August.

In adulthood, I've paid the price by fighting a propensity for skin cancer, but my West Texas summers were spent, as much as possible, without a shirt. The object was to end up with the darkest tan in our neighborhood gang. By December, it would be only a memory, but on the Fourth of July, it was a measure of male accomplishment.

Summers were a time for breakthrough, a time for doing new, daring and different things. I learned to swim during the vacation days after Muleshoe opened its public pool. It was on a hot July day that I rode my bicycle all the way from the top of the hill near the high school football stadium to our house on West 5th Street, without touching the handlebars. It was on a summer afternoon that I successfully parallel parked our family Ford and went home with a Texas driver's license.

Making summer the time to do something for the first time started early with me. I was born on July 10, 1936. The habit is one that I've never tried to break; instead, I've cultivated it. On a June day in 1957, I went straight from my college exams to board a TransTexas DC-3 for a flight to Dallas's Love Field, logging the first of hundreds of thousands of air miles. My wife, Robbie, and I were married on August 25, 1958.

It was on summer days that I first stood on the Equator in Kenya, cruised the Nile to Murchison Falls in Uganda, saw the pyramids in Egypt, gazed down from the heights of Masada in Israel, explored the coliseum in Rome, was awed by the Alps in Switzerland, strolled the Champs Élysées in Paris, was overwhelmed by the Grand Canyon, marveled at the raging waves of the Pacific Ocean along Oregon's coast and saw the wild majesty of our Rocky Mountains. Under full moons, on summer nights, I've seen North Dakota's Mt. Rushmore, Rio de Janeiro's Sugar Loaf Mountain and the Acropolis in Athens.

Summertime brought me my first tastes of watermelon, iced tea, homemade ice cream, fried catfish, coffee boiled over a mountain campfire, peach cobbler, Eskimo Pie® and frosted root beer. While fighting July heat, I learned that RC Cola® went with Moon® Pie, that salted peanuts added zest to Coca-Cola® and that there was an advertised excuse for drinking Dr. Pepper® three times every day. During the first summer after Six Flags Over Texas opened in Arlington, I joined our son, Rob, in experiencing the adrenalin rush of the initial drop of a really good roller coaster. We've both been hopelessly addicted ever since.

It was on the last night of a 1947 revival at the Church of the Nazarene in Hamlin, Texas, that I (borrowing from my maternal grandfather's vocabulary) "got saved." It was during a summer revival at Muleshoe's First Baptist Church that I felt God's call to preach. It was on the Fourth of July, 1976, our country's 200th birthday, that I spoke to a capacity crowd at Virginia State College's football stadium in Petersburg, Virginia.

Summer is indeed a time for new experiences. I never want to stop anticipating that. Since turning 60, I've added a few more summer "firsts," including cruising the Amazon River and seeing the rain forests of Brazil.

Not too long ago, an 80-plus grandmother graduated from Harvard. Both Paul Harvey and George Bush skydived after they were 70 years of age, and John Glenn returned to space at the age of 77. Is there something you have always wanted to see, taste or experience? Why not pick a pretty summer day and do it? Don't ask anyone's opinion before you act. They might tell you to act your age. Summer is the time for things to grow and bloom. Seize the day! Sing a new song, write a poem, paint a picture, take a trip, go online, ride a camel or grow a mustache. September is coming, but during July and August, you may still have the best day of your life.

When is Old?

HOW DO YOU KNOW IF YOU ARE GETTING OLD?
Is it when every story you've heard, you've told?
Is it when what hair you have is gray?
Is it when loose neck skin is there to stay?

Are you old when you remember then, not now?
Is it when to operate high tech, a child must show you
    how?
Is it when you remember gay apparel for the straight,
And marriage for life with one mate?

How do you know you're getting old?
Is it when you can read only what's big and bold?
Is it when a computer must count the calories you
    avoid and the pills you take?
Is it when there are some postures you just can't fake?

WHEN IS OLD?

It all depends, whether old is age and physical ability,
Or attitude and mental agility.
Is it faddish acceptance that you require,
Or dreams alive and a heart on fire?

Arrogant youth says there's nothing left that you can do.
They say, "Step aside and let me through."
But stand your ground; it's not too late
Your song to sing and your mark to make.

You're old when you think you are,
When you fold your tent and lose your star.
For now, there are dreams to chase and work to do.
Make anyone run who follows you.

Father Knows Best

ONE OF THE FIRST THINGS I CAN REMEMber being certain about was that my father knew everything. He didn't tell me that, and of course it wasn't true, but nothing in my childhood would have convinced me otherwise.

Reflection has caused me to realize that I was observing a man with more than his share of common sense, who was an avid reader and who spent years absorbing the pontificating of barber shop politicians, philosophers and theologians. Add to that the skills acquired growing up on a dryland farm during the Great Depression and, later, building our house. No wonder I can seldom remember seeing him stumped by a task or subject.

After I became a teenager, we had radical disagreements. This was especially true of politics. He was greatly distressed when I showed early signs of straying from the party of FDR and the New Deal. I'll never forget the storm when he found the reply to a letter I had written to a young senator of the opposing party. In spite of this, I never lost my respect for his grasp of history and his ability to discern character. He could smell a fake a mile away.

Observing my father taught me two things about acquiring and sharing knowledge. First, a smart husband reads the *Reader's Digest* to his wife. During 36 years of marriage, my mother must have heard, "Did you know that..." or "Listen to this" a jillion times.

This is one lesson that I have learned well. Actually, I've taken it a step farther. I not only read the *Reader's Digest* to my wife, Robbie; I also make sure she never has to trouble herself with reading the comics or editorials from the daily newspaper. Like it or not, she is up to date on the standings of every professional sports team, and she is fully informed about anything that has ever had any effect on any Canadian rat.

How in the world does an unmarried woman ever learn anything? If she marries well, a girl is assured of a well-rounded education. Any husband worth his salt will see to that.

I've never told my wife this, but I suspect that God built the compulsion to read out loud into husbands as a way of saving them from abysmal ignorance. Whether Robbie has paid any attention to any of the bad jokes or home safety tips that I've read to her, I've learned a lot. I can't get away from the sneaky feeling that I've been the victim of the mental equivalent of Tom Sawyer getting someone else to paint his fence.

After years of diligent commitment to the education of my mate, I belong to that legion of disillusioned husbands who have discovered that their reading aloud is not really appreciated. My own voice sounds so good to me; how in the world could it possibly get on someone else's nerves? Why would anyone want to see and read something for themselves when they can have it served up to them while they are slaving over a hot stove or ironing shirts?

Husbands were information superhighways years before anyone went online, and the variety has always rivaled anything available while surfing the Internet. What wife could fail to be overwhelmed by learning that snake oil cures ingrown toenails in remote Asian villages, or by being told that if you see a turtle on a fence post, it didn't get there by itself?

In spite of this, wives demonstrate a total disregard for the blessing of having husbands who can and do read out loud. More often than not, while their mates are attempting to bring them up to date on major league batting averages, the mothers of our children are crawling into hours of close-mouthed retreat working crossword puzzles.

One poor unappreciated man fell under the wrath of a wife who had put up with more than enough from her fountain of knowledge. Wanting to know at least one thing first, she drove from Muleshoe to the monthly horse auction in Clovis and bought a donkey. When her husband came home that night, he found the animal munching hay from the family bathtub.

When he stormed into the kitchen announcing, "There's a donkey in our bathroom," his wife calmly looked up from clipping grocery coupons and said, "I already knew that."

Aggie Jokes:
Been There, Heard That

I F YOU WANT TO SPEND THE REST OF YOUR
life fighting a losing war, take on changing the
fact that most of what we find funny is at somebody else's painful expense. To the constant frustration of folks who take themselves and everybody else
too seriously, joke writers will be the last people to
line up and march in step with the politically correct
guardians of modern utterance.

Now, don't get me wrong. Only a crude, slow-
thinking, mean-spirited cretin, with zero self-esteem,
gets his jollies from telling or hearing jokes that spin
off somebody else's race or physical handicaps. Laughing at your own expense is something else. Three of
the funniest people that I know are deaf, dyslexic and
spastic. I don't find any humor in their conditions,
but they do, and they make me laugh.

Growing up in a small-town barber shop exposed me to just about every joke known to man. Add to that my addiction to radio comedians of that era, such as Bob Hope, Jack Benny and Red Skelton, the slapstick flicks of The Three Stooges, Bud Abbott and Lou Costello and the animated antics of Tom and Jerry, Bugs Bunny, Daffy Duck and Elmer Fudd, and you get a good fix on my humor orientation. As a boy, the words I heard most often were, "Did you hear the one about...?"

Early on, I figured out that some stuff was lewd, rude and crude, better off having never been heard and never to be repeated. I also decided that some people are fair game. Why?

First, because they are just too high-profile to ignore. Secondly, their careers, institutions and competitions leave them wide open. Thirdly, people take shots at them not because they are weak, but because they are strong. In my daddy's Muleshoe barber shop, if you asked ten people to make a list of those who were most often the butts of their jokes, these groups would have made all ten: lawyers, politicians, preachers, cowboys, grandparents and Texas Aggies. Since I followed in my grandfather's footsteps and became a preacher, I've spent my adult life being on the receiving end of a lot of humor. I've always believed that if you can't take it, don't dish it out.

Having said all of that, there are some folks who have broad shoulders and who walk in positions of strength who still might be justified in pleading for mercy. For instance, I've always marveled at the courage it takes to live in Texas Tech territory and have a bumper sticker that says, "My son is a Texas Aggie."

I can't imagine the abuse that has been endured by Dr. Frank Pollard, a Texas A & M graduate who is pastor of the First Baptist Church in Jackson, Mississippi. He responds to his tormentors by grinning and saying, "When I was at A & M, we told idiot jokes; now idiots tell Aggie jokes."

A good friend, who is a successful A & M graduate, says that he doesn't mind hearing people joke about his alma mater because of what they call an Aggie five years after his graduation: "boss."

When was the last time you heard a new Aggie joke? I guess that depends on how old you are. Probably the oldest one begins with the question, "How many Aggies does it take to change a light bulb?" The correct answer is, "Three; one to hold the bulb and two to turn the chair."

To grow up in Texas during the heyday of the old Southwest Conference was to learn to take your best shots against your team's arch rivals. This resulted in an overload of Texas A & M versus University of Texas jokes. The one I heard most often when I was in high school was about the freshman at College Station who was being initiated into the Cadet Corps. He was told to go to Austin and find out why the Longhorns tell so many Aggie jokes.

He had hardly walked onto the UT campus when someone recognized him as an Aggie. A threatening mob backed him up against the school's landmark tower and demanded to know what he was doing so far from home.

"The Cadet Corps made me come up here to find out why you tell so many jokes about us," he stammered.

A big Texas interior lineman said, "That's easy. It's because you are so stupid."

"How can you say that?" challenged the Aggie.

Smiling, the Longhorn raised his right hand in front of the tower's brick wall. With his open palm facing the A & M fish, he said, "Hit my hand." When the angry spy swung a clenched fist, the Texas football player simply dropped his hand.

With his right hand in a cast, the poor Aggie returned to College Station. Immediately, he was surrounded by upperclassmen demanding to know why people in Austin tell so many Aggie jokes. "Let me show you," said the freshman. Holding his left hand in front of his face, he said, "Hit my hand."

No one that I know finds more joy in telling Aggie jokes than Dr. Bill Tanner, a retired Baptist denominational leader and university president. Because of this, you can imagine my surprise to find him full of sympathy after the A & M campus was struck by a disastrous storm. With a grave expression, he reported that the wind and hail did $2 million worth of improvements.

Hearing their rivals talk, you'll conclude that Aggies are accidents looking for places to happen. Six graduate students were riding in a pickup truck when it ran into a lake. The two young men who were in the cab escaped, but, tragically, the four in the back drowned. They were unable to get the tailgate down.

Now, I'd feel bad about telling these stories if I didn't know two things. One, some of you will stop the next person you see to tell him or her an Aggie joke. Two, it's just a matter of time until one of my Aggie friends tells someone, "Last Sunday, Wayne dreamed that he was preaching, and when he woke up, he was."

Can You Say That in English?

WHEN I WAS A STUDENT AT MULESHOE High School, if someone had asked me, "What language do you speak?" I would have given them a quizzical look and replied emphatically, "English." Today, I would say, "English, but not exactly."

This came home to me several years ago when I was visiting a school in Kenya, a former English colony. I was accompanied by my good friend, Mike Richardson, a former newspaper editorial writer (now an author) with a masterful vocabulary. A student stopped him in the middle of a sentence and, speaking with a crisp British accent, said, "Please, sir, if you will speak English, I can understand you."

As I listened, I remembered a London pastor who quoted George Bernard Shaw: "The people of America and England are divided by a common language." He had gone on to say, "I like to visit in the United States because, even though you do not speak English, you understand a little of it."

I spend a part of each year in Brazil. While I struggle to learn Portuguese, I am embarrassed by that nation's young people as they excel in their English studies. Even as I congratulate them on their accomplishments, I think how frustrated and confused they will be when they finally make their first trips to the United States. Can you imagine them trying to converse with a good ole boy from Alabama or a teenager from Los Angeles and thinking, "Oh, no—I've been studying the wrong language."

Language is a living thing, and each of us communicates through a verbal montage that reveals our distinctive heritages. Without thinking, we pepper our talk with words we can't exactly explain but which make perfect sense to everybody in our bailiwick.

As a boy, I would often question one of my parent's colorful expressions, and my mother would say, "Oh, that's just an old Eddard's saying."

Not only did that not explain anything, I've never even been able to find out what that meant. My wife, Robbie, says that her folks said the same thing, and her mother thought that it originally was "an old Edward's saying," or an adage from an early reading textbook. Whatever their origin might be, I reckon I'd be plumb tongue-tied if it wasn't for a head full of "old

Eddard's sayings." Out of my West Texas learning, there is one for every occasion.

My daddy had a way of putting things that got your attention and gave whatever he said just the right nuance. He didn't cuss, but we knew what he meant when he hit his thumb with a hammer and muttered, "Sam Pat and little pistols!"

We never failed to get the picture when he described something leaving in a hurry by saying, "It took off like a shot cat through the peach orchard."

When he was totally baffled, "Well, I'll be hornswoggled!" seemed to say it all.

While I can't remember Daddy or Mother ever telling my brother and me "Good night," their "Sleep tight and don't let the bedbugs bite" always seemed like good advice.

Before I knew anything about the Old Testament book of Proverbs, my young mind was chock-full of my father's homespun wisdom, things he had been told by his father and uncles:

"There's more than one way to skin a cat."
"Don't count your chickens before they hatch."
"There's no fool like an old fool."
"Don't bite off more than you can chew."
"Don't get caught napping."
"Keep your shoulder to the wheel, your nose to the
      grindstone and your ear to the ground. Now, try
      to work in that position!"
"Don't let folks rub you the wrong way."

"Don't let anybody get your goat."

"Look before you leap."

"Don't look back; somebody might be gaining on you"
    (a quote from Satchel Paige, the great baseball
    pitcher).

"Don't get in over your head."

"Don't get sucker-punched."

"Keep your cotton-picking hands in your own lap."

"Smile, and people will wonder what you've been up to."

"If you see a light at the end of the tunnel, it might be
    a train."

"A bird in the hand is worth two in the bush."

"Don't get your dander up."

My mother used her West Texas colloquialisms to add color and punch to her already unique vocabulary. If somebody was putting on airs and acting a little too hifalutin', she'd put them in their place by saying, "She thinks that she's the cat's meow." When oil was discovered on the property of one of her childhood friends, Mother described the woman's elevated position by saying that she was living in high cotton and eating high on the hog. She might describe a drugstore cowboy strutting out of Daddy's barber shop as "a ding-dong daddy from Dumas who thinks he's God's gift to women."

Mother's ways of putting things pop up in my talk every day:

"Nervous as a long-tailed cat in a room full of rocking
  chairs."
"Fidgety as a cat on a hot tin roof."
"Cold as a well digger's nose."
"Cold enough to freeze the horns off of a billy goat."
"Trapped between the devil and the deep blue sea."
"Caught between a rock and a hard place."
"Mean as a junkyard dog."
"Sad enough to make a moth bawl."
"Oh, fiddlesticks!"

I've always been quick to confess that my heroes
have always been cowboys. This is why my best memories of wisdom and expressions come from hanging
out with my grandfather and some of his old ranch
hand cronies. Thankfully, their language is alive and
well in West Texas sale barns and in the lyrics of Riders In The Sky and Baxter Black.

"Keep both feet in the stirrups and don't spit into the
  wind."
"Never look straight up at a bird."
"Now the fat's in the fire!"
"That's a bunch of hogwash."
"She's as pretty as a new calf in a field of clover."
"He just cocked his head and looked at me like a calf
  looking at a new gate."
"Don't drink downstream from the herd."
"Don't squat with your spurs on."
"Never change horses in midstream."

"Don't buy a pig in a poke."

"Don't look a gift horse in the mouth."

"You can lead a horse to water, but you can't make him drink."

"If you can't run with the big dogs, stay on the porch."

"Would you cut me a little slack?"

"He thinks he's got the world by the tail on a downhill drag."

Just when I think that North Americans have a corner on "old Eddard's sayings," one of my Brazilian friends will be challenged by a lack of resources and baffle me with a strange Portuguese expression. When I ask what that means, he will smile and say, "If you don't have a dog, hunt with your cat!"

More to Say About Sayings

I N THE PREVIOUS CHAPTER, I WROTE ABOUT
what my mother called "old Eddard's sayings." I
reckon I thought that I might be the only person
thinking about such stuff, but wouldn't you know, I've
been proven wrong. One other time I thought I was
wrong about something, but I was mistaken.

I called my old Muleshoe High School buddy, Billy
Ellis, hoping he would join me in congratulating me
on the originality of my particular nostalgia. Instead,
he carried on about the column his wife, Carol, had
just written for the *Friona Star*. It seems that she had
this bright idea about digging into the origins of old
sayings.

As if I needed somebody else to make me feel like
a copycat who was just standing around saying, "me,
too," I picked up a copy of the Raleigh, North Carolina, *News & Observer* on my way through the Ra-
leigh/Durham airport. There on page one of section C

was G. D. Gearino's column entitled "Lessons In the Fine Art of Folk Talk."

Now, I'm thinking that I must have been in the middle of "National Old Sayings Month," and somebody just forgot to tell me. Just to keep the ball rolling, my wife, Robbie, and I came up with a list on eight legal size pages. Here are a few:

When you thought you were on the verge of winning an argument or making a point, somebody may have waved you off by saying, "Oh, your grandpa's mustache!"

My daddy used to deflate my exaggerated expectations about something I had found by saying, "Shoot, that ain't worth a plugged nickel." That always left me wondering how you'd go about plugging a nickel. Since I never figured that out, I settled for making sure that I never took any wooden nickels, although I've always hoped I'd get to see one.

A talkative kid like me didn't hear it much, but when my mother was trying to solve some household mischief and asked, "Who did this?" I did hear her follow that up a few times with, "Did the cat get your tongue?" I guess my reluctance to volunteer too much information came from hearing the World War II warning, "Loose lips sink ships."

Back during the days before air conditioning, it was pretty common to hear folks talk about it being "hotter than a firecracker." Even with my childish way of figuring things out, I decided early on that the heat of a July day had nothing to do with some women being called "red hot mamas."

After joining two or three buddies in trying a pinch of Skoal®, I could never understand why anybody would describe a great piece of pie at Gladys' Coffee Shop as being "gooder'n snuff." Observing the stained lips and utter contentment of some of my grandmother's churchwomen friends, I did know what folks were talking about when they saw somebody get riled and said, "Oh, she's just out of snuff."

Then there was the explanation for not being able to get going mentally and physically, "I'm not feeling up to snuff today."

Every kid anxious to get off to the picture show, rodeo or church pie supper heard a slowpoke parent say, "Hold your horses," or "Keep your shirt on." If the frustrated child dared to stick his bottom lip out, he would be told not to "get bent out of shape." Still pouting behavior at the event would be explained by saying, "He just got up on the wrong side of the bed this morning."

To me, that was ridiculous since my bed was pushed up against a wall, and I had only one choice about which side to get up on.

When I was a kid, there was a description for about every physical or mental condition:

"Tough as a boot."
"Ugly as mud."
"A face that would stop a clock."

"Pretty as a picture."

"Slow as Christmas."

"Fast as greased lightening."

"Easy as pie."

"Easy as falling off a log."

"Hard as a rock."

"Slick as calf slobbers."

"Clean as a whistle."

"Clear as a bell."

"Busy as a bee."

"Smart as a whip."

"Sharp as a tack."

"Cute as a button."

"Flatter'n a flitter."

"Snug as a bug in a rug."

"Dog tired."

"Mad as an old wet hen."

"Tuckered out."

Well, I reckon if you've been thinking about some of this same stuff lately, you've been "reading my mail."

Actually, you can make up your own "old Eddard's sayings," and nobody will be the wiser. They'll just think that's something they slept through. G. D. Gearino in Raleigh even came up with some instructions on how to do this. He suggested that "anyone can develop a knack for colorful and obscure sayings, providing you follow a few simple rules.

"First, try to make reference to either a domestic animal, a vegetable or a common agricultural implement. This establishes you as an earthy, canny sort, wise to fundamental truths in the way only men and women of the soil are.

"Second, connect that animal, vegetable or tool to some equally earthy activity.

"Third, make your animal/vegetable/tool-based activity relate in an obscure, but seemingly meaningful, way to the topic at hand. Do this in a confident and folksy tone of voice."

Gearino suggested that a good time and place to try this out would be when you're called on at work to review a half-completed project. Suppose "someone suggests some midstream adjustments—stupid ideas, really, but what do you expect from those jokers from headquarters—so everyone turns to you for your opinion. This is when you snap into action.

"'Well,' you say, 'if you're stewing tomatoes, you don't fiddle with the heat.'

"You won't hear anything else out of them. While they're pondering, grab the last doughnut."

Enough Said

MY DADDY USED TO CATCH ME HAMMER-ing away at something that had proven to be a pretty good way of doing things and he'd say, "Sonny, be careful and don't ride a good horse to death."

How many times have you seen a pitcher watch a ball sail over the center field fence and heard a sports commentator say, "He went to the well one time too many."

Maybe an old actor has lost his zip and somebody sums it up by saying, "He stayed too long at the fair."

Of course, there's another side to the coin, "If it ain't broke, don't fix it."

Or, as Darrell Royal used to say, when coaching the University of Texas football team in a championship game, "Dance with them that brung you."

Still, I reckon I've just about worn out this "old Eddard's saying" business. I promise, when I get this load off the wagon, I'll whistle a different tune.

My wife, Robbie, who is pretty good at telling me how the cow ate the cabbage, says that if I'm bound and determined to trot this same old horse out again, I'd better keep what I say short and sweet (which reminds me of a high school cheerleader that I used to know, but that's another story, and I'm about to dig a hole I can't get out of).

I'm smart enough to know that it's a good idea to look before you leap. That brings to mind the three Bailey County crows that ate their fill of some old lunch meat that had been thrown out by a ranch cook. Full as ticks, they perched on a pump handle to savor their good fortune. Before long, one of them said, "Would you look at the time! I'd better skedaddle before my wife decides to fix my wagon." One of his buddies said, "Write if you get work." The bloated bird flapped off, struggled to gain altitude and took a nosedive into the dirt. Shaking his head, one of the crows still gripping the perch asked, "When is old Corny gonna learn not to fly off the handle full of baloney?"

Somehow, I've got to get off this sayings kick before I lay an egg, slip a cog, jump the rail, go down the drain or hit the wall. I guess for the past two or three times out of the chute, I've been taking the easy way home because coming up with new stuff is no walk in the park. Sometimes it has me climbing the walls. I always want to hit a home run, but I'm more apt to strike out or be thrown out stealing. When it comes time for us to touch base, I don't want to throw you a curve; so I promise that, instead of letting you die on base, I'll go down swinging. If you don't want to play that game, we'll have to decide if we're going to punt or go for it.

I don't ever want to be accused of being over the hill or around the bend. I would always rather fly high than to lay low. Before I buy the farm, I'll bite the bullet and go for broke. In my opinion, it's better to be up a tree and out on a limb than down for the count. If you give it your best shot, you may end up flying high and rolling in clover.

Sure, when you really want to go to town and you haul off and take a shot in the dark, you run the risk of somebody thinking you're not playing with a full deck or that your elevator doesn't go all the way to the top. Instead of letting sleeping dogs lie, go ahead and stir up a hornet's nest. When you scratch where it itches, you just might hit the nail on the head and come out smelling like a rose. Then, instead of whistlin' Dixie, you'll be seen as lean an' mean, flyin' high and cookin' with gas.

Has it ever struck you a little strange that we humans are the superior species, but when we want to come off looking real good, we compare ourselves to birds or animals? We use phrases such as:

"Smart as a fox."
"Strong as an ox."
"Bold as a lion."
"Busy as a beaver."

"Hungry as a bear."

"Meaner than a junkyard dog."

Sometimes it's pretty hard for us to live up to these comparisons. Like the 90-year-old caddie who bragged to a dubious golfer that he had eyes like an eagle. He said, "I've been a caddie at this club for 70 years, and I've never failed to see where a ball went."

On the first tee, the golfer hit a terrible slice into the trees. "Did you see where that went?" he asked.

"Sure, I did," replied the caddie. "I've got eyes like an eagle."

"Well, where is it?" asked the golfer.

Scratching his head, the old man said, "I don't remember."

Autumn Leaves

FOR THOSE OF US WHO TEND TO WALLOW in nostalgia, autumn has to be the most sentimental season. My mind is flooded with memories when I hear any rendition of Kurt Wiell's "September Song." A calendar photo of New England fall foliage causes me to immediately mellow out.

Growing up on the South Plains of West Texas, I always figured that somebody was just making up those pretty pictures. In the first place, I didn't believe that there could be that many trees in one place; and if there were, there was no way they could look that spectacular. Visiting in Groton, Connecticut, during an October week showed me just how wrong I had been.

While my autumn memories aren't dramatizations of Norman Rockwell paintings, they frame some of my best childhood days. Change a little scenery, and they're probably not too different from yours, even though you may have grown up in Virginia or Oregon.

My brother and I knew that summer was over when Mother arranged for a shopping spree that focused on fall clothes and school supplies. For a kid, those forays into every variety, clothing and shoe store on Muleshoe's Main Street were a blend of delight and torment. I liked few things better than buying new school supplies. I liked few things less than being forced to try on clothes that conformed to adult opinions about what looked good on me and would allow me some "growing room."

Getting school supplies always involved negotiations with Mother over what was necessary and what was wanted with a passion. The necessary list included Big Chief tablets, pencils, a bottle of that messy amber glue with a slotted rubber nipple, and an eraser that left little balls of soft rubber scattered all over the arithmetic that I was sure to foul up. The really wanted stuff included a zip-up notebook binder with lots of neat inside pockets, a big box of Crayolas®, a plastic whatchamacallit that doubled as a ruler and guide for drawing a wild variety of geometric designs and, of course, a fountain pen.

Fountain pens were a joy to buy and a terror to use. To start with, they came in a dazzling variety and offered endless engineering promises. As a third grader, clutching a new pen and a bottle of blue ink caused me to fantasize about getting an early start on writing the great American novel. In reality, I left big blots on numerous pages of homework, ruined the pockets of shirts that I had not wanted in the first place, and kept the index finger and thumb of my right hand looking like I worked in a dye factory.

Clothes were predictable. My mother had a thing for corduroy. She thought it looked good, wore well and was warm, the big three in buying school clothes. To me, it was heavy and scratched the insides of my young thighs raw. This, and the fact that its swishing sound made it impossible to slip up on a classmate, caused me to spend many school days walking bow-legged.

Blue jeans caused a real dilemma. I liked them and they were necessary. It was impossible to impersonate Gene Autry without a pair of Levi's® with a big, turned-up cuff. The problem was breaking in a new pair of those suckers with the brass buttons. It took an extra hour to get ready for school just squirming and straining through the fastening process. Once that was accomplished, a teacher could be sure that the number of restroom breaks requested by boys had been greatly lessened. Going through getting in and out of those pants two or three times in a day would leave any cowboy plumb tuckered out.

Getting back to school meant that football season was under way, another sure sign that summer was over. My first autumn football memories include us grade school kids being bussed over to the old field on the north side of town to watch the Yellow Jackets go to war against Sudan, Morton, Littlefield or Olton.

By the time I finished the eighth grade, the team had moved to new grass west of the new high school. By the time I graduated, they were the Mules. The Friday-night rituals of marching bands, leaping cheerleaders and charging padded knights never changed. September was always born full of hope. October usually ended with the same old disappointment against Sudan.

During my school days, autumn in Bailey County meant that it was cotton-picking time. I knew the fields were ready when I heard Daddy launch into his annual explanation of the difference in picking cotton and pulling bolls. I was never sure that I had it down right, but one or two trips to a farmer's patch convinced me that I wanted to keep my cotton-picking hands as far away from that work as possible.

A lot of my classmates didn't have any choice. When I was in the first, second and third grades, school turned out for cotton picking every year. Back in those days, big families were necessary if all the work was to get done. Every farm kid knew that autumn meant dragging a cotton sack for long, back-breaking hours. Now, air-conditioned harvest machines have made all that a distant memory.

When the *Muleshoe Journal* ran a picture of a proud farmer standing beside the county's first bale of cotton, we knew that the first frost was overdue. Now it was fall sure enough!

Although we lacked autumn foliage around Muleshoe, we never lacked a couple of other traditional fall symbols, wild geese and ducks. We were on their route from Canada to the Gulf of Mexico, and they loved our grain fields. We added to them our own unique winter citizens, the thousands of Sand Hill cranes that populated Coyote Lake.

While hunting ducks, quail and pheasants was a fall passion for hundreds of West Texas men, and while it was just a short drive to good deer country, it took a little more effort to participate in the manly pursuit of bigger game. This meant getting the crops in, loading up with five or six other buddies and hightailing it for the Rocky Mountains in Colorado. One of these trips supplied enough war stories for a year's worth of visits to gin offices, seed stores and barber shops.

Five good ole boys from out around the Hub community had made such a trip to a remote campsite. While four of them settled in with chili, strong coffee and playing cards, one was eager to get on with the hunt. He said, "I'm gonna see what's in them woods. Y'all can waste your time layin' 'round here if you want to."

About an hour later, his friends heard frantic whoops and the sound of crashing brush. Suddenly their wild-eyed comrade burst through the cabin's front door and made a dash for the back door. A riled-up bear was on his heels. As he slammed the door in the animal's face, he yelled, "Skin him, boys, and I'll go get another one!"

Just Call Me Tex

O
UR FAMILY MOVED FROM LUBBOCK,
Texas, to Virginia in 1982, then to Oklahoma
in 1986. You'd think that more than enough
time has passed to get Texas out of my system, but it
just hasn't happened. To paraphrase an old axiom,
you can take the boy out of Texas, but you can't take
Texas out of the boy.

For a while, I thought that my affections and loy-
alties had been transferred with my mailing address,
but then I kept spending autumn Saturday afternoons
trying to find out how the Texas Tech Red Raiders had
come out on the gridiron. When I watched the Weather
Channel on TV, I couldn't get away from being interested in what was in store for Amarillo and Lubbock.
When cross-country trips took me through Dallas/Fort
Worth airport, I couldn't help grabbing and devouring
a copy of *Texas Monthly*. The surest sign that a big
part of me hadn't moved was the office tension that

came from the fact that a majority of my Virginia co-workers were rabid Washington Redskins fans. I had a great secretary, but there were some things we just didn't talk about when her team was playing my Cowboys.

Moving to Oklahoma was pretty humiliating for a hopeless Texan. Here they have cards showing a map of Texas and Oklahoma with the caption "Oklahoma is still on top." Only one thing has come easy for me about the rivalry between these two states. It's been plumb natural to back the Sooners when they go to the Cotton Bowl to take on the Longhorns. Growing up in West Texas, my two favorite football teams were Texas Tech and whoever was playing the University of Texas that Saturday.

In 1997, two things reinforced this "once a Texan, always a Texan" thing. One was an article in the October issue of *American Cowboy* magazine about the origin of Wolf® Brand Chili. I read that as if I had discovered a long-lost piece of my family history. When we left Texas, it didn't take long to discover that nobody east of Texarkana has any idea what real chili is supposed to taste like. Everybody I grew up with knows that it's supposed to taste like a "big, thick, steamin' bowl of Wolf® Brand Chili." And, I might add, with no beans!

The other reminder of how little I've gotten away from my native traditions was my emotional response to *Texas Monthly*'s "Around The State" segment about the annual high school football grudge match between the Midland Lee Rebels and the Odessa Permian Panthers. One of the reasons that we have cable TV is so that I can watch Texas high school scores on Fox's Southwest Sports Channel. I still can't close the book on a Saturday until I know how the Muleshoe Mules did the night before. My good friend, Bill Ellis, thinks I'm equally interested in the fortunes of his Friona team. I suspect that he passes on only the good news.

Excuse the arrogance, but traveling to five continents and most of our United States has taught me something about why Texas comes in for so much gibing and jabbing. I think it's for the same reasons that folks cheer against a sports powerhouse, knock a successful business, undermine a hero or harass the student who excels. Exposure to strength and achievement makes most folks downright uncomfortable. Increasingly we are encouraged to settle for being average, which is the best of the worst and the worst of the best. Folks can't handle the confident self-image that says, "Go ahead. I can take any shot you can fire."

That's Texas—big, brash and proud. When it's true, why deny having the prettiest girls, the toughest boys, the biggest ranches, the most oil wells, the best chili and the proudest traditions? Why, if you melted all that ice and snow around Alaska, Texas would still be the biggest state in the U.S.A.

Sure, I know that all of that flies in the face of anybody who wasn't conceived, born and raised in Texas. That's why there are as many Texas jokes as there are Aggie jokes. Think about it—all those poking-fun stories have a big grain of truth tucked away in them. That's what galls somebody who has no idea how to pronounce Mexia.

For example, I've known many a wheeler-dealer who was the inspiration for the story about the Texas businessman who dashed out of New York's Kennedy Airport, jumped in a waiting taxi and yelled, "Let's go!"

"Where to?" asked the cabbie.

"Anywhere, son. I've got business everywhere!" came the reply.

My personal favorite has always been the response of the Texan who was shown Niagara Falls and told, "You haven't got anything like that where you come from."

Smiling, he agreed and added, "But I know a plumber in Fort Worth that could fix that for you in about half an hour."

Just when somebody is ready to sell a Texan short, he might do well to remember the East Coast girl who became enamored with a slow-talking ole boy who had drifted a far piece from his home pastures. She asked, "Being from Texas, do you have any oil wells?"

"No, ma'am," he said. "I don't reckon I do."

"Well, do you have any cattle?" she asked.

"No, ma'am, I don't reckon I do."

"What do you have?" she wanted to know.

"Well, ma'am," he drawled. "I've got this little spread that covers about 40 acres."

Startled, the girl asked, "Is that all?"

Humbly, the Texas boy said, "Yes, ma'am, I reckon it is."

"Just what do you call this little place of yours?" she wanted to know.

Scratching his head, the grinning Texan said, "Well, the best I can recollect, they're callin' it downtown Dallas."

Writing all of these stories has given this old Texas boy a chance to do some old-fashioned lyin' and braggin', the kind of stuff I was trained for in my father's barber shop, in the halls of Muleshoe High School and during Saturday nights of cruising Main Street in Clovis. I'm getting to do what folks say you can't do. I'm getting to go home again.

As long as I live, wherever I am in the world, when someone asks where I'm from, I'll proudly say, "Muleshoe, Texas." When they laugh and call me "Tex," I sure won't be offended. I'll just grin and be thankful that I've got a legitimate claim to the title, unlike the old boy from Louisiana who went by "Tex" because he didn't want to be called "Louise."

Things That I Remember

T HE THINGS WHICH I REMEMBER MOST,
Float through my mind like friendly ghosts.
Clothed in aroma, panorama and sound.
With each new year, they more abound.

1. The bark and waggle of my first dog, Bo.

2. Daddy's crumbling toast in my over-easy eggs.

3. The captivating height of Muleshoe's water tower.

4. Surviving my first prohibited adventure, the two-block walk to Daddy's barber shop.

5. The fascinating risk of watching red ants close up.

6. The marvel of holding a baby horned toad in my hand.

7. Watching cowboys drive a herd of cattle through Muleshoe to the railroad's loading chutes.

8. The enchantment of seeing a *real* cowboy, Johnny McMurtry.

9. Smelling Jeris® Hair Tonic in Daddy's shop.

10. The smell of menthol as Daddy removed a hot towel from the face of a shave customer.

11. The great taste of brown sugar sneaked from Mother's cabinet.

12. The taste of dried apricots sneaked from Mother's cabinet.

13. Hot Ralston® for breakfast on a cold winter morning.

14. Curly Bradley selling Hot Ralston® over the radio as Tom Mix.

15. Neat stuff for a quarter and a Hot Ralston® box top.

16. Radio heroes: Hop Harrigan and Sky King; Sergeant Preston of the Yukon and his wonder dog, Yukon King; The Lone Ranger and Tonto; The Green Hornet; Captain Midnight; Jack Armstrong, the All-American Boy; Superman; and Tom Mix.

17. Radio fun: Amos 'n' Andy, Fibber McGee and Molly, Red Skelton and his many characters,

Duffy's Tavern, The Great Gildersleeve, Burns & Allen, Henry Aldrich, Our Miss Brooks, Bob Hope, Lum 'n' Abner, Minnie Pearl and Rod Brassfield.

18. Singing cowboys: Gene Autry, Roy Rogers, Jimmy Wakely and Rex Allen.

19. Straight-shooting, hard-hitting, no-nonsense cowboys: Bill Elliot and Bobby Blake as Red Ryder and Little Beaver, Hopalong Cassidy, Charles Starrett, Randolph Scott, Johnny Mack Brown, Gilbert Roland as the Cisco Kid and The Duke, John Wayne.

20. Radio adventure: Humphrey Bogart and Lauren Bacall in "Bold Venture," "Inner Sanctum," "Your FBI," "The Shadow," "Sam Spade" and "Gunsmoke."

21. Movie horror: The Cat People, Spider Woman, Frankenstein's monster, vampires, werewolves, zombies and the wrath of disturbed mummies.

22. Great crime fighters: Charlie Chan, The Thin Man, Boston Blackie, Dick Tracy, Batman and Robin, Captain Marvel, The Phantom, Flash Gordon, Zorro, The Black Whip and The Durango Kid.

23. Movie memories: *Lassie Come Home, My Friend Flicka, Thunderhead, National Velvet, Gone With the Wind, High Noon, The Wild One, Blackboard Jungle, Rebel Without a Cause, The French Line,*

Three Coins in the Fountain, Thirty Seconds Over Tokyo, Casablanca, The Greatest Show on Earth, White Christmas, Holiday Inn, An American in Paris, Cabin in the Sky, A Tree Grows in Brooklyn, For Whom the Bell Tolls, Flying Leathernecks, Miracle on 34th Street, Harvey, From Here to Eternity, Two Years Before the Mast, War and Peace, The Hunchback of Notre Dame, The Yearling, The Maltese Falcon, and Sergeant York.

24. Books: *Lassie Come-Home, My Friend Flicka, Thunderhead, Green Grass of Wyoming, Smoky, The Cow Horse, Wildfire, Riders of the Purple Sage, The Rainbow Trail, The Call of the Canyon, The Longhorns,* Will Rogers' autobiography, *Ben Hur, Black Beauty, Robinson Crusoe,* the Hardy Boys adventure series, the Bobbsey twins series, biographies of Daniel Boone, Abraham Lincoln and George Washington, *The Adventures of Tom Sawyer, The Adventures of Huckleberry Finn* and *The Call of the Wild.*

25. Sports heroes: Doc Blanchard and Glenn Davis, Johnny Lujack, Bob Feller, Ben Hogan, Joe Louis, "Slinging" Sammy Baugh, Doak Walker, John David Crow, Joe DiMaggio and Rocky Marciano.

26. People I wanted to be like: Bill Stern, the sports announcer; Fred Harman, who drew "Red Ryder"; Will James, a cowboy writer and artist; and Billy Graham.

Music I can't forget: "Stardust," "September Song," "Autumn Leaves," "Sentimental Journey," "Chattanooga Choo Choo," "Little Brown Jug," "In The Mood," "I Wonder Who's Kissing Her Now," "My Desire," "Blue Moon," "Tuxedo Junction," "Baby, It's Cold Outside," "White Christmas," "Rudolph, The Red-Nosed Reindeer," "Singing In The Rain," "Your Cheatin' Heart," "San Antonio Rose," "T's For Texas," "Frankie and Johnnie," "Harbor Lights," "Don't Sit Under The Apple Tree With Anyone Else But Me," "Don't Fence Me In," "The Cattle Call," "My Adobe Hacienda," "Along The Navajo Trail," "Back In The Saddle Again," "Happy Trails," "When It's Round-Up Time in Texas," "When It's Springtime In The Rockies," "The Strawberry Roan," "Tumbling Tumbleweeds," "(I Love You) For Sentimental Reasons," "Misty," "Mule Train," "Shake, Rattle and Roll," "Peggy Sue," "Allegheny Moon," "Don't Be Cruel," "Heartbreak Hotel," "Blue Suede Shoes," "Blueberry Hill," "Mood Indigo" and "Moments To Remember."

27. Memories I would rather not have: Two Christmases in a hospital, seven months in bed, doing the first grade twice, watching my own IVs, the taste of alcohol on a thermometer, looking away and feeling the prick of a needle, fighting nausea and cramps, legs too weak to walk, the taste of iron tonic, the taste of cod liver oil, the taste of cherry cough syrup, the heat and vapors of a hot

menthol chest poultice, the taste of crushed aspirin, waking on sheets wet from night sweats and the taste of hospital-prepared Malt-O-Meal®.

28. Words I can still hear: Cotton John, at 5 a.m. over KGNC in Amarillo, saying, "Good morning. This is the best part of the Golden Spread day!" (Then, I didn't believe it.) The announcer at the bus station in Lubbock, reciting the names of all the places a person could go. To name a few, Slaton, Post, Snyder, Roscoe, Sweetwater, Abilene, Cisco, Ranger, Jacksboro, Fort Worth and Dallas. The rodeo announcer at the Texas Cowboys Reunion in Stamford, "Next, out of chute number six, a hand from the Four Sixes Ranch, Cody Hightower, on a bronc named Bad Medicine.... Well, he got off sooner and harder than he planned. Give him a good hand, folks; it's all the pay this cowboy will be gettin' today."

Every day I try to remember just how blessed I am in having memories that I never get tired of recalling. I can join Bob Hope in saying to my hometown, parents, grandparents, teachers and friends, "Thanks for the memories!"

Acknowledgments

ALL OF THE STORIES YOU HAVE JUST READ flow out of a childhood that was blessed by people who loved, nurtured and protected me. Everyone around me fed my imagination and encouraged me to laugh and dream. So, first I must acknowledge the debt that I owe to those that I can no longer thank personally, my maternal grandparents, Reverend Samuel J. and Josie King, and my parents, Mabel and Clinton Bristow. Many of the stories in *18 Miles From Earth* are their stories.

Thankfully there are many to whom I'm indebted that I can thank personally. These include, R. L. and Beth Sigrest, who said a thousand times, "You've got to put these in a book."

A special "thank you" to Gary and Lisa Taylor of Jackson, Tennessee. Once again, they have backed up words with deeds and have helped in a very practical way to make this project a reality.

My best friend in high school was Billy Ellis. Now, he is a successful newspaper publisher. He affirmed the worth of the stories, published several in his papers and wrote the foreword for this book. Of course, his wife, Carol, has her own book crying to be published. I can hardly wait for you to read *Memories on Maple Street*. Someday, Carol...

Steve Shirk, my singing friend with an outrageous sense of humor, prompted more than one of the jokes in the book. Old groaners, every one!

Mike Richardson, the one person besides my wife that I can always count on to tell me the truth, said, "You can write." I believed him.

My brother, Reverend James Dudley Bristow, kept reminding me of things that I would have missed. Someday we will get together long enough to pool our memories, then that will be a whole new book.

Magann Rennels owns Gil Lamb Advertising and a popular cable television outlet in Muleshoe, Texas. She is the daughter of Gil Lamb, one of the men who instilled in me a fierce pride and love for my hometown. For many years, he was the owner and voice of Muleshoe's only radio station, KMUL. Magann heard one of my stories and asked me to do a weekly program over her Channel 6. My two and one-half years of writing and recording those "Sentimental Journey" programs gave me the bulk of this book. I'm grateful to her for allowing me to "go home."

ACKNOWLEDGMENTS

My greatest debt is owed to my companion, lover, encourager and best friend—my wife, Robbie. None of these stories would have been written if she had not read the first one and said, "Keep on."

Since then, she has been constant in her encouragement. She has laughed at the oldest jokes, offered the best criticism, been the guardian of my grammar and spelling, and put up with my being a kid again. She researched and validated things that I vaguely remembered. She typed the manuscript and proofread every word. Without her, there would have been no beginning or end to this.

Together, Robbie and I want to thank our son, Rob. We want him to have good memories, and we didn't want him to miss the things that made our lives richer. In reality, if no one else ever reads these stories, it will be O.K., because they were really written for Rob.

Wayne Bristow
June 2000